For Jes

with

Muse & Sal
xx

How to Live

A guide to the
Christian Journey

Stephen Cottrell
Steven Croft

CHURCH HOUSE
PUBLISHING

First published under the title Travelling Well in 2000 by
National Society Enterprises Ltd
Second edition published in 2003 by Church House Publishing.

Church House Publishing
Church House Great Smith Street
London SW1P 3AZ

This edition published in 2011 by Church House Publishing

The opinions expresssed in this book are those of the authors
and so not necessarily reflect the official policy of the General
Synod or the Archbishops' Council of the Church of England.

British Library Cataloguing in Publication Data

A catalogue record for this book is available from the British
Library

ISBN 0 7151 4240 0

Printed and bound in Great Britain by Ashford Colour Press

Contents

Acknowledgements

The publisher gratefully acknowledges permission to reproduce copyright material in this book. Every effort has been made to trace and contact copyright holders. If there are any inadvertent omissions we apologize to those concerned and undertake to include suitable acknowledgements in all future editions. Page numbers are indicated in parentheses.

Unless otherwise stated, scripture quotations are from The New Revised Standard Version of the Bible copyright © 1989 by the Division of Christian Education of the National Council of Churches in the USA. Used by permission. All rights reserved.

Other published sources include the following:

The Archbishops' Council of the Church of England: *The Prayer Book as Proposed in 1928* **(87)**; *The Christian Year: Collects and Post Communion Prayers for Sundays and Festivals* 1997 **(12, 34, 37, 98, 110)**; *Common Worship: Daily Prayer*, 2002 **(34–5)** *Common Worship: Initiation Services* 1998 **(6, 7, 8, 12)**; *Common Worship: Services and Prayers for the Church of England* 2000 **(1, 5, 10, 21, 51, 54–6, 89, 90, 130, 131)**; all of which are copyright © The Archbishops' Council of the Church of England.

Cambridge University Press: Extracts adapted from *The Book of Common Prayer* (1662), the rights in which are vested in the Crown in the United Kingdom, are reproduced by permission of the Crown's Patentee, Cambridge University Press **(33, 37, 44, 110)**.

Darton, Longman & Todd Ltd: Anon, *Rule for a New Brother*, copyright © 1973 and 1986 and used by permission **(31–2, 58)**; Robert Durback (ed.) *Seeds of Hope: A Henri Nouwen Reader*, copyright © 1989 and 1998 and used by permission **(96)**.

Darton, Longman & Todd Ltd and Les Editions du Cerf: Scripture quotation taken from *The New Jerusalem Bible*, copyright © 1985 and used by permission **(85)**.

The English Language Liturgical Consultation: English translation of the Apostles' Creed prepared by the English Language Liturgical Consultation, based on *Praying Together*, copyright © ELLC, 1988 **(9)**.

Episcopal Church of the USA: *The Book of Common Prayer* according to the use of the Episcopal Church of the USA, 1979. The ECUSA Prayer Book is not subject to copyright **(119)**.

The European Province of the Society of St. Francis: 'A Song of the Word' from *Celebrating Common Prayer: The Daily Office SSF* (Mowbray, 1992) copyright © 1992 & 1996 **(45)**.

Hodder & Stoughton Limited: Extracts from William Abraham, *The Logic of Evangelism* 1989 **(107)** and Frank Colquhoun (ed.), *Contemporary Parish Prayers* 1975 **(57–8, 66)**. Reproduced by permission.

Kingsway Publications: Extracts from Dick Williams (ed.), *More Prayers for Today's Church* (Kingsway, 1984). Copyright © R. H. L. Williams 1972, 1984 and used by permission **(88, 128)**.

Kingsway's Thankyou Music: Matt Redman, 'I will offer up my life'. Copyright © 1994 Kingsway's Thankyou Music, PO Box 75, Eastbourne, East Sussex, BN23 6NW, UK. Used by permission **(96)**.

Methodist Publishing House: Extract from *The Methodist Service Book* copyright © 1975 Trustees for Methodist Church Purposes and used by permission **(95)**.

Missionaries of Charity, Calcutta: 'Dear Lord, help me to spread thy fragrance' from *In the Silence of the Heart*, comp. Kathryn Spink (SPCK, 1983) **(105)**.

Janet Morley: 'O God, I try and think about you' from *Prayers for Children* (Kingfisher, 1988). Copyright © Janet Morley and used by permission **(118)**.

Penguin UK: Extracts from St Augustine, *The City of God*, translated by Henri Bettenson (Penguin Classics, 1972) copyright © Henry Bettenson, 1972; Julian of Norwich, *Revelations of Divine Love*, translated by Clifton Wolters (Penguin Classics, 1966) copyright © Clifton Wolters, 1966; Thomas à Kempis, *The Imitation of Christ*, tranlated by Leo Sherley-Price (Penguin Classics, 1982) copyright © Leo Sherley-Price, 1952 **(121, 128, 129)**.

SPCK: George Herbert, poem beginning 'Prayer the Church's banquet, Angel's age' from *The Country Parson, The Temple*, edited by John W. Wall (SPCK, 1981) and used by permission **(35)**.

Stuart Thomas: Prayer of forgiveness from *New Patterns for Worship* (Church House Publishing, 1995). Copyright © Stuart Thomas, 1989 and reproduced by permission **(21)**.

Westcott House, Cambridge: 'Lord, you feed us' from *New Patterns for Worship* (Church House Publishing, 1995) copyright © Westcott House, Cambridge **(44)**.

Wild Goose Publications: 'These I lay down' from *Love From Below* (Wild Goose Publications, 1989), words and music by John L. Bell and Graham Maule, copyright © 1989 WGRG, Iona Community, 840 Govan Road, Glasgow G51 3UU, Scotland **(119)**.

World Library Publications: Extracts from *Come Lord Jesus* by Lucien Deiss copyright © 1976, 1981, Lucien Deiss, published by World Library Publications, Schiller Park, IL 60176. All rights reserved. Used by permission **(57, 77)**.

How to use this book

Travelling Well is a companion for your Christian life. We've written it mainly for people who have recently completed a short course learning what it means to be a Christian and have been baptized or confirmed or made an affirmation of faith as an adult. We hope it will also be a useful companion to those who have been Christians for a longer time.

Our aim has been to give you some help and resources for the next part of the journey.

Each short chapter provides an introduction to the theme to guide you and then a selection of readings and prayers.

The sections can be tackled in any order. We've begun the book with a chapter on what it means to be baptized, based around the words of the service and one about the lifelong business of being changed by God. There are then four chapters on the inner journey, exploring prayer, the Scriptures, Holy Communion and belonging to the Church. Then four chapters on what we have called the outer journey: seeking the kingdom; faith in daily life; serving God and Christian witness. At the end you will find two final chapters: one for times of difficulty and the last on Christian hope.

Both of us have been privileged to walk alongside other people as they have begun their Christian journey at different times and in different places. This book is, in part, the fruit of those experiences.

May God give you grace to travel well on the great Christian journey.

Stephen Cottrell

Steven Croft

Preface by the Archbishop of York

If we reflect on our human relationships, especially those with people to whom we are very close, we recognize that their characters change over time. The pressure to talk at great length about all manner of things can pass naturally into a depth of communication where words are fewer, though laden with shared meaning.

As we reflect on our relationship with God, we will also be aware of such changes. Sometimes this can be disorientating. A pattern of prayer that once seemed to bring a great deal of help and comfort can come to seem somehow unfulfilling. The sort of worship we find uplifting can begin to change. Aspects of ourselves that once felt uncomfortable begin to trouble us and we feel called to deeper change and conversion.

These changes are natural. Jesus called us to perfection (Matthew 5.48) but as Cardinal Newman reminds us, 'to obtain the gift of holiness is the work of a life'.

It is a work in which we seek to cooperate more and more fully with the Holy Spirit as he seeks to make Christ ever more present to us, and changing us in the process. It is my hope that *How to Live* will be of help to you as you seek to respond ever more deeply to God's call in your life and will assist you at those times when the outer or inner journey can seem perplexing, as well as when it is deeply joyful and consoling.

✠ David Ebor

Foreword

Christianity is not just a list of things to believe in. The Christian faith is really the Christian life. All the things we believe about God, and all the things we believe about the world and human life, and how in Christ the relationship between the two has been restored, only really make sense when they become part of the lives we lead. Because of our faith in Christ we inhabit the world in a different way. The journey oflife which seemed to end in death is now a holy pilgrimage which ends, as it began, with God, in life. And the way we travel through life changes. We are no longer isolated individuals, but sisters and brothers, members of a single humanity, inhabiting the precious oasis of a single world. The way we care for each other and the way we care for the world changes. So as people discover the Christian faith they must also discover the Christian life; and for many people who are not yet Christian, it will be seeing this new life lived out each day, in the church and in the world, which will be the very best advertisement for Christianity.

So this is a book to help you travel well. It explores the big themes ofthe Christian journey, enabling readers to visit the inner and outer journeys of Christian discipleship. Indeed, we have given it a new name: *How to Live*.

It is our hope that Christian people can find here a book that will help them deepen their commitment to Christ, and their practice of the Christian faith. As bishops in the Church of England we have the great joy of confirming lots of people each year. We believe this is a book that would be ideal for newly confirmed young people and adults, and also for those who have completed a nurture course like Alpha or Emmaus. But we also dare to hope that any Christian who wants to let the Christian faith become part of their everyday life will find this book an encouraging help, something they can return to again and again. In this way, the things we believe in can become the things we do. Developing patterns of Christian behaving and responding, we can make the Christian faith the loom upon which the fabric of our life is woven, a life lived in harmony with God and thirsting for God's kingdom to be seen on earth.

Stephen Cottrell

Steven Croft

1
Beginning the Way

Our Lord Jesus Christ has told us
that to enter the kingdom of heaven
we must be born again of water and the Spirit,
and he has given us baptism as the sign and seal
   of this new birth.
Here we are washed by the Holy Spirit and made clean.
Here we are clothed with Christ,
dying to sin that we may live his risen life.
As children of God, we have a new dignity
and God calls us to fullness of life.

Common Worship: Holy Baptism (Introduction)

> Do you not know that all of us who have been baptized
> into Christ Jesus were baptized into his death? Therefore
> we have been buried with him by baptism into death, so
> that, just as Christ was raised from the dead by the glory
> of the Father, so we too might walk in newness of life.
>
> Romans 6.3-4

A different journey

Every journey to faith in Christ and every story of faith is different.
Each person is unique and special, created in the image of God. Your
journey and your story are your own. For some people, the journey of
faith begins when they are children. There is never a time when they
do not believe and that faith grows, stretches and changes as they
mature to adult life. Others are brought up and believe within the
family of the Church as children but then rebel or perhaps just drift
away (like the younger son in Jesus' parable in Luke 15). Later in life,
through the grace of God, they find their way home by many
different roads. An increasing number never have the opportunity
to learn about Christian faith as children or young people and
consciously begin to seek God as adults.

For some the journey back to God and coming to faith can be
sudden and dramatic: powerful moments of discovery and turning
round like Saul's encounter with the risen Christ on the road to
Damascus. For others, perhaps the majority, there is a more steady
and gradual road to travel, like Simon Peter's travelling with Christ
throughout his ministry, to the cross and beyond. In everyone's
journey *learning* about Christian faith will play some part. *Other
Christians* will have welcomed and befriended you and encouraged
you in your search. There will have been a growing awareness
of a *relationship with God* developing as you pray and begin to
be changed.

Out of all these different threads of learning, community, prayer,
of past experiences, present encounters and future hopes, a unique
tapestry is being woven which is the story of your own faith: God's
dealings with you and your dealings with God. Your own story finds

its place within the larger story of God's dealings with his people through the centuries as told in the Bible and continued in the story of the church.

We each need to make sure we can reflect on and treasure the story of our own faith. If you have not already done so, you may want to write your story down as a reminder to you in the years to come of what God has done. Many Christians find it helpful to keep a journal from time to time, writing down both their experiences and Bible passages and prayers which have been helpful.

A single sign

Whatever your journey to faith and whatever your story, every Christian at some point in that journey passes through the waters of baptism: the sign and the seal of new birth in Christ. Some are baptized as young children. When they come to the point of making an adult declaration of faith they are not baptized again but make their baptismal promises on their own behalf either in a service of confirmation or (if they have been confirmed as children) in a service of Affirmation of Baptismal faith. Others are baptized as adults, normally as part of a service which also includes confirmation.

Baptism is a sign for the Christian which is rich in meaning for the whole of our Christian lives, not simply a single event which marks our entry into the church. Jesus himself was baptized in water by John at the beginning of his public ministry. At the end of Matthew's gospel we read of the risen Christ's command to his followers:

> Go therefore and make disciples of all nations,
> baptizing them in the name of the Father and of the Son
> and of the Holy Spirit and teaching them to obey
> everything that I have commanded you.
>
> Matthew 28.19

The Book of Acts testifies to the way in which the Early Church followed this command of Christ: men and women respond to the good news of Jesus Christ and response involves repentance, faith and being filled with the Holy Spirit, all symbolised through baptism. Time and again the letters in the New Testament call each generation of Christians to live out the truth of their baptism:

> There is one body and one Spirit, just as you were called to the one hope of your calling, one Lord, one faith, one baptism, one God and Father of all . . .
>
> Ephesians 4.4-5

> . . . when you were buried with him in baptism, you were also raised with him through faith in the power of God, who raised him from the dead.
>
> Colossians 2.12

We begin this companion to the Christian life by thinking about baptism. The words and actions of the baptism service hold important truths not only for the way we begin our Christian lives but for the way we go on living them out. It may be that you have recently been baptized or confirmed yourself and the service is fresh in your mind. Or else you may have been baptized many years ago and need to be reminded of what that baptism means. The following sections draw on the words of *Common Worship: Services and Prayers for the Church of England.*

Turning around

As candidates come for baptism, surrounded and supported by family and friends and by the wider church, they are asked to declare publicly that they turn away from all they know to be wrong:

> Do you reject the devil and all rebellion against God?
> **I reject them.**

> Do you renounce the deceit and corruption of evil?
> **I renounce them.**

> Do you repent of the sins that separate us from God
>   and neighbour?
> **I repent of them.**

This public turning away is a once and for all promise for the whole of our lives. Yet, because we are not made perfect we will often be drawn or tempted back into our old ways. We will need from time to time not only to remember our baptismal promises but to renew them privately and sometimes publicly.

The word 'conversion' means turning round. Turning round means turning away from something – but also turning towards something or, rather, someone, else. And so the candidates are also asked:

> Do you turn to Christ as Saviour?
> **I turn to Christ.**

> Do you submit to Christ as Lord?
> **I submit to Christ.**

> Do you come to Christ, the way, the truth
>   and the life?
> **I come to Christ.**

Dying to Live

Christ is the centre of the Christian faith. In these words we promise to be disciples of Christ for the whole of our lives. Following that solemn promise, in a service of baptism, the candidates declare their faith in the words of the Apostles' Creed, printed at the end of this chapter. Then each candidate is baptized in water and in the name of the Father, the Son and the Holy Spirit.

The water in the service is a sign and symbol of many things. Water reminds us of God's activity in creation, of refreshment and new life; of God's rescue of the nation of Israel from slavery in Egypt to freedom in the promised land. Water is a sign that we are washed clean from all sin and made new. Water is a sign that our old self, our former life, dies with Christ and we are reborn to new life with him, life which will continue after we have physically died. In many churches, those who are baptized as adults are immersed fully in water: a sign of complete cleansing as well as of death and rebirth. In some the candidates will be dressed in new white robes as a sign of their new life in Christ and the new beginning which has been made.

Filled with the Holy Spirit

In the confirmation service at this point the Bishop prays that each person will be filled with the Holy Spirit, to be strengthened to live out the promises each has made in baptism. Jesus promises the gift of the Holy Spirit to every Christian: we cannot live the Christian life or declare Jesus as Lord without God working within us through the Spirit.

> Let your Holy Spirit rest upon them:
> the Spirit of wisdom and understanding;
> the Spirit of counsel and inward strength;
> the Spirit of knowledge and true godliness
> and let their delight be in the fear of the Lord.

The gift of the Holy Spirit is not a once and for all event: a charging up of the batteries which is meant to last for the whole of our lives. It is much better to imagine a continuous filling of the Holy Spirit. As we give out to others, so we need to be renewed and replenished by God. Paul tells the Ephesian Christians to 'go on being filled with the Spirit'. Jesus speaks of the Holy Spirit as a river of living water flowing through the believer.

Commissioned to serve

Those who are baptized are called to worship and to serve God.
Baptism and membership of the Church carry responsibilities.
Following their baptism (and/or confirmation), each Christian is
asked another series of questions in which they are commissioned
for ministry:

> Will you continue in the apostles' teaching
>   and fellowship,
> in the breaking of bread, and in the prayers?
> **With the help of God, I will.**

> Will you persevere in resisting evil,
> and, whenever you fall into sin, repent and
>   return to the Lord?
> **With the help of God, I will.**

> Will you proclaim by word and example
> the good news of God in Christ?
> **With the help of God, I will.**

> Will you seek and serve Christ in all people,
> loving your neighbour as yourself?
> **With the help of God, I will.**

> Will you acknowledge Christ's authority over
>   human society,
> by prayer for the world and its leaders,
> by defending the weak, and by seeking peace
>   and justice?
> **With the help of God, I will.**

The Christian life has a basic rhythm, or heartbeat, of coming
together with others in worship and of being sent out to share
in the mission of God to the whole of creation. The words of the
commission invite you to share in this rhythm by participation in
fellowship and worship and by engagement in Christian witness,
service of others and seeking to build the kingdom of God.

Living out your baptism

Baptism, or Confirmation, or an Affirmation of Baptismal Faith marks a significant point in any Christian journey – but each is a new beginning rather than an ending. If you have recently been baptized or confirmed, this is the point to commit yourself in new ways to disciplines of prayer and worship. This is a God-given opportunity to begin to live out your faith in meaningful ways. Seek God's call for the life he has entrusted to you.

As we travel on we do not leave our baptism behind us. We move forward by living in and with our baptism. We remember each day that we have been washed and cleansed and forgiven. We remember each day that we have been given the gift of a new identity and a new nature in Christ. We remember each day that we are called to die to ourselves and live a new life in Christ.

From time to time as we share in the baptism of other people, we are powerfully reminded of our own baptism, of the promises we made and of the new life we have begun. The same happens as we enter a church building and see the baptistry or the font. Even a simple act like washing in the mornings can be a reminder of the truth that we are baptized members of the Body of Christ called to live in and through him. The remainder of this book will help you to understand more of what it means to live out your own baptism into Christ.

God has delivered us from the dominion of darkness and has given us a place with the saints in light.

You have received the light of Christ;
walk in this light all the days of your life.
**Shine as a light in the world
to the glory of God the Father.**

Readings and prayers

The Apostles' Creed

I believe in God, the Father almighty,
creator of heaven and earth.

I believe in Jesus Christ,
his only Son, our Lord,
who was conceived by the Holy Spirit,
born of the Virgin Mary,
suffered under Pontius Pilate,
was crucified, died, and was buried;
he descended to the dead.
On the third day he rose again;

he ascended into heaven,
he is seated at the right hand of the Father,

and he will come to judge the living and the dead.

I believe in the Holy Spirit,
the holy catholic Church,
the communion of saints,
the forgiveness of sins,
the resurrection of the body
and the life everlasting. Amen.

Common Worship

The Easter Anthems

Christ our passover has been sacrificed for us:
so let us celebrate the feast,
not with the old leaven of corruption and wickedness:
but with the unleavened bread of sincerity and truth.
Christ once raised from the dead dies no more:
death has no more dominion over him.
In dying he died to sin once for all:
in living he lives to God.
See yourselves therefore as dead to sin:
and alive to God in Jesus Christ our Lord.
Christ has been raised from the dead:
the firstfruits of those who sleep.
For as by man came death:
by man has come also the resurrection of the dead;
for as in Adam all die:
even so in Christ shall all be made alive.

Common Worship: Canticles (based on 1 Corinthians 5.7,
Romans 6.9 and 1 Corinthians 15.20).

Dear Lord and Father of mankind
forgive our foolish ways!
Re-clothe us in our rightful mind,
in purer lives thy service find,
in deeper reverence praise,
in deeper reverence praise.

In simple trust like theirs who heard
beside the Syrian sea,
the gracious calling of the Lord,
let us like them without a word,
rise up and follow thee,
rise up and follow thee.

O Sabbath rest by Galilee!
O calm of hills above,
where Jesus knelt to share with thee
the silence of eternity,
interpreted by love!
interpreted by love!

Drop thy still dews of quiteness,
till all thy strivings cease;
take from our souls the strain and stress,
and let our ordered lives confess
the beauty of thy peace,
the beauty of thy peace.
Breathe through the heats of our desire
thy coolness and thy balm;
let sense be dumb, let flesh retire;
spaek through the earthquake, wind and fire,
O still small voice of calm!
O still small voice of calm!

John Greenleaf Whittier

When you went down into the water, it was like night
and you could see nothing; but when you came up
again it was like finding yourself in the day. That one
moment was your death and your birth: that saving
water was both your grave and your Mother.

Font inscription in Portsmouth Cathedral,
from St Cyril of Jerusalem

Today God has touched you with his love
and given you a place among his people.
God promises to be with you
in joy and in sorrow,
to be your guide in life,
and to bring you safely to heaven.
In baptism God invites you on a life-long journey.
Together with all God's people
you must explore the way of Jesus
and grow in friendship with God,
in love for his people,
and in serving others.
With us you will listen to the word of God
and receive the gifts of God.

Common Worship: Holy Baptism (Commission)

Collect for Easter Day

Lord of all life and power,
who through the mighty resurrection of your Son
overcame the old order of sin and death
to make all things new in him:
grant that we, being dead to sin
and alive to you in Jesus Christ,
may reign with him in glory;
to whom with you and the Holy Spirit
be praise and honour, glory and might,
now and in all eternity.

Common Worship: Collects
and Post Communions

2
Being Changed

To grow is to change. To have become perfect is to have changed often.

John Henry Newman

Above all, clothe yourselves with love, which binds everything together in perfect harmony. And let the peace of Christ rule in your hearts.

Colossians 3.14,15

We live in a world that bombards us with images of who we should be and what we should look like. From our clothes to our lifestyle, from our personality to our shape we are confronted with images of what it is to be attractive and desirable and asked if we measure up. And if we don't then we must change. We must strive after the image. We must become the person we desire. We must fight that flab, pump that iron, buy those clothes, lift that chin, climb that ladder. If I work hard I can create myself.

The Christian faith is also about change. But the liberating good news is that I am set free from striving to be someone else. I can stop chasing after the empty glamour of that image which seduced me. I can stop denigrating myself, and stop wishing I were different. Instead, I can become myself. After all, this is the one person I am capable of becoming! Me, as God intended. But this involves the greatest change of all. It involves a complete re-orientation of life, because to find myself as God intended I must first lose myself. I must stop worrying what the world says I should look like or act like, and worry about what God says instead. What kind of person does God want me to be? This is the important question that begins the lifelong process of transformation that makes up the Christian pilgrimage. This transformation God brings is not about becoming someone else; it is about becoming yourself.

God has a picture in his heart of what each one of us can be. The work he does within us is like that of a picture restorer, revealing beneath the dirt and the grime the beautiful picture that is already there. It is the image of Christ that dwells within. And it strips away all the false images that so easily allure. Sometimes this will be dramatic and exposing; more often it will be tender and cleansing. Always it is about understanding myself in relation to others. Jesus' own summary of the law and the prophets is about true love of self, true love of neighbour and true love of God. These three cannot be separated. As I am changed into a person who is capable of such loving so I become the person God intended, and so I am made ready for heaven. We call this changing, holiness. It is a hard and beautiful road. But it does not depend on our effort. It depends on letting God love us, and letting God change us.

So how does this happen? Mostly it is about our attitudes and our growing relationship with God. We discover our true self in relationship with him. This inner transformation then overflows into a changed life.

I am made in the image of God

This is the first truth about human beings. And it changes the way I think about myself. It is no longer so easy to put myself at the centre of life, for the life I enjoy depends on God. Therefore I must look to God if I want to become properly myself. My prayer, my fellowship within the Church, my reading of Scripture, the nourishment I receive in the sacraments – all the things we are exploring in this book – these are the things that will enable me to draw upon God and be shaped by him.

This also changes my relationship with others. Every human being is both uniquely individual and a part of the whole. Every human being is worthy of the same dignity and rights that I desire for myself. Every human being shows me something of God.

I am a child of God

Jesus called God 'Daddy'. I am not just made in the image of God I am a beloved child. The astonishing claim of the Christian faith is that God cares for me. He is interested in me. He loves me. And if this is true for me, it is true for everyone. Therefore everyone is my brother or sister regardless of creed, or colour, or class.

I am made for community with God

Because my life is deeply rooted in God I can no longer conceive of 'myself' as an entirely separate entity. In fact I cannot be fully myself without God. I am made for community. Firstly with God, but also with those around me and with the whole creation of which I am a part. And just as God has taken the initiative in creating me his child, so also he has taken the initiative in making this community possible. Because of what God has done in Jesus Christ we are reconciled to him and to one another.

If I want to be redeemed from slavery to self then I must put on Christ. I must let go of self – meaning that bewitching tendency to always put self first – and find my true self in Christ. Here I can find the forgiveness, the peace and the acceptance that I am longing for. Here I can stop pretending to be someone else. I can take off all the masks. I am completely known. I am completely loved. I can be forgiven.

All this means taking sin seriously. Because of what Jesus has done for me, I know that I am reconciled to God. But despite this I still persist in putting self first. So I cut myself off from God and from others. In my prayers I need to seek God's forgiveness regularly. Sometimes this may well mean making a formal confession of sin. Always it means that I must be ready to forgive others and to try and show humility, patience and love in all dealings. (We are in grim solidarity when it comes to the isolating effects of sin.) But in Christ I am shown the way to my true self and therefore the way back to other people and to God.

I need to live in the knowledge of God's mercy. God longs for me to come to him. He has already done everything, which is necessary in order for me to have life with him. When I acknowledge my need of him and take one small step in his direction, he takes a mighty leap towards me. His arms are always outstretched – to suffer for me and to receive me.

I am part of Christ's body

This also shows me the true nature of the Church. God has made the first move in bringing reconciliation; all he asks is for us to respond. What is the Church, but the community of people who have responded?

Thus Paul describes the Church as being Christ's body (1 Corinthians 12.27): not a human institution, but the community of those who belong to Christ.

I am a temple of the Holy Spirit

This new community with God and this new relationship with others, is all the work of the Holy Spirit. When we live our lives in community with God the Holy Spirit makes his dwelling with us. This change manifests itself in many different ways. Some Christians record dramatic experiences such as speaking in tongues – a kind of heavenly language that gives people a new freedom to praise God. Others quite literally fall over with the overwhelming sense of God's love and power. But we should not feel overlooked or alarmed if we have not had these experiences. The Bible consistently reports that the highest gifts of the Spirit are faith, hope and, above all, love. These are things the Holy Spirit will bring to us all, if we ask. So, we do need to pray for the Holy Spirit to come afresh into our lives. And we should not try to limit or predict quite how this will be exhibited in us.

What we can be sure of is that the Holy Spirit is the one who comes from God. We receive fresh assurance that we are loved by God who is our Father. We receive fresh experience of our redemption through Jesus. Just as the Holy Spirit heard the response of Mary to the invitation of God and conceived Jesus within her, so the Holy Spirit waits to hear our response and longs to come and form Jesus in us. This is the faith, hope and love we can be sure of.

I am a co-heir with Christ

Finally this inner change whereby Christ is put at the centre of my life confronts me with the glorious paradox of Christian faith. I put Christ at the centre of my life, and he puts me at the centre of his! This is what Jesus means when he says we will find our lives by losing them (Mark 8.35).

The vows of the wedding service, when man and woman are joined as one flesh, capture the spirit of how Jesus gives himself to us: 'All that I am I give to you, and all that I have I share with you.'

Paul describes this by declaring that 'when we cry "Abba, Father!" it is the Spirit bearing witness that we are children of God, and if children, then heirs, heirs of God and joint heirs with Christ' (Romans 8.16,17).

I am a citizen of heaven

In other words our belonging to Christ changes the orientation of our life. My life is no longer a journey which ends in death – it is believing this which deceives me into thinking that accumulating status and possessions for myself is the way to happiness – my life is a pilgrimage which ends with God. I am a citizen of heaven. My true home, just like my true self, is to be found in God. But, because God has come to meet me in Jesus and show me the way home, heaven is not just the destination that awaits me at the end of life, it is a present reality pervading all I think and do and say. Therefore I am called to live my life now by the standards and values of God's kingdom.

The standards of God's kingdom are given in the Ten Commandments (Exodus 20.1-17). Here I can find foundations for the way I live. The Ten Commandments are the bedrock of Christian morality.

The values of God's kingdom are given in the Beatitudes (Matthew 5.1-10). These are slightly more difficult to understand. At first sight it appears that God's injunction to poverty of spirit and meekness of heart is an invitation to let people walk all over us. But to be poor in spirit means to be open to God; to mourn means to lament for the pain and injustice of the world; to be meek means to be obedient to God's will; to hunger and thirst for righteousness means to have a vision for how the world should be; to be merciful means to give from the abundance that God has given to us; to be pure in heart means to see to the heart; to be peace-makers means going beyond the resolution of conflict to the creation of harmony and reconciliation; to be persecuted for righteousness' sake means plainly that this being changed into the likeness of Christ and living by his values carries a price. The world will persecute and hate us; because the values of God's kingdom stand in splendid contrast to the values of every age and every human society.

But each of these values also carries a blessing. If we live with openness to God then we shall receive God's kingdom now. If we cry out against injustice we will receive comfort, which is the strength to persevere. If we are obedient to God's will then we shall prevail. If we hunger for righteousness we shall be put right with God. If we are

merciful to others we shall receive mercy ourselves. If we are pure in heart we shall see God and know his purpose. If we seek peace then we are truly God's children. Even when we are persecuted, even in the darkest hour when we see the terrible
consequences of human sinfulness and it seems as if the world has conquered, the kingdom of heaven will still be ours. God has not promised us that it will be easy following Jesus. Indeed, the
. first thing Jesus gives his disciples is a cross to carry. But if we submit ourselves to God and allow him to change us then we shall be blessed.

This journey from beloved child to joint heir and citizen of heaven is the way of holiness, a constant re-dedicating of our life to God, a constant refining of our self so as to be made ready for heaven. It involves an inner journey – nourishing the inner spiritual life through prayer, the reading of Scripture, the sacraments, worship and fellowship of the Church – and an outer journey – expressing Christian faith through a changed, fully human, Christian life. The next two sections of this book explore these two journeys. But always in this life we must remember it is about travelling well – not imagining we have yet arrived. To be changed into the person God wants us to be takes a lifetime. But by happy coincidence that is precisely how much time each one of us has been given.

Readings and prayers

The Ten Commandments

> Then God spoke all these words: I am the Lord your God, who brought you out of the land of Egypt, out of the house of slavery; you shall have no other gods before me.

> You shall not make for yourself an idol, whether in the form of anything that is in heaven above, or that is on the earth beneath, or that is in the water under the earth. You shall not bow down to them or worship them; for I the Lord your God am a jealous God, punishing children for the iniquity of parents, to the third and the

fourth generation of those who reject me, but showing steadfast love to the thousandth generation of those who love me and keep my commandments.

You shall not make wrongful use of the name of the Lord your God, for the Lord will not acquit anyone who misuses his name.

Remember the Sabbath day, and keep it holy. For six days you shall labour and do all your work. But the seventh is a Sabbath to the Lord your God; you shall not do any work – you, your son or your daughter, your male or female slave, your livestock, or the alien resident in your towns. For in six days the Lord made heaven and earth, the sea, and all that is in them, but rested the seventh day; therefore the Lord blessed the Sabbath day and consecrated it.

Honour your father and your mother, so that your days may be long in the land that the Lord your God is giving you.

You shall not murder.

You shall not commit adultery.

You shall not steal.

You shall not bear false witness against your neighbour.

You shall not covet your neighbour's house; you shall not covet your neighbour's wife, or male or female slave, or ox, or donkey, or anything that belongs to your neighbour.

Exodus 20.1-17

The Beatitudes

Blessed are the poor in spirit, for theirs is the kingdom of heaven.
Blessed are those who mourn, for they will be comforted.

Blessed are the meek, for they will inherit the earth.
Blessed are those who hunger and thirst for
righteousness, for they will be filled.
Blessed are the merciful, for they will receive mercy.
Blessed are the pure in heart, for they will see God.
Blessed are the peacemakers, for they will be called
children of God.
Blessed are those who are persecuted for
righteousness' sake, for theirs is the kingdom
of heaven.

Matthew 5.3-10

Prayers of confession and forgiveness

Father eternal, giver of light and grace,
we have sinned against you and against our neighbour,
in what we have thought,
in what we have said and done,
through ignorance, through weakness,
through our own deliberate fault.
We have wounded your love,
and marred your image in us.
We are sorry and ashamed,
and repent of all our sins.
For the sake of your Son Jesus Christ,
who died for us,
forgive us all that is past:
and lead us out from darkness
to walk as children of light.
Amen.

Common Worship

May the God of love
bring us back to himself,
forgive us our sins
and assure us of his eternal love
in Jesus Christ our Lord. Amen.

Patterns for Worship

21

A prayer of faith and trust

Father,
I abandon myself into your hands;
do with me what you will.
Whatever you may do, I thank you:
I am ready for all, I accept all.
Let only your will be done in me,
and in all your creatures –
I wish no more than this, O Lord.
Into your hands I commend my soul;
I offer it to you with all the love of my heart,
for I love you, Lord, and so need to give myself,
to surrender myself into your hands
without reserve,
and with boundless confidence,
for you are my Father.

Charles de Foucauld, *Prayer of Abandonment*

Examination of conscience

A simple and effective way of examining your life in the light of the
gospel is to read through 1 Corinthians 13, and whenever it says
'love' simply substitute your own name. This, and a regular reflection
on the Beatitudes and the Ten Commandments, keeps us realistic
about ourselves and our need for God.

You shall love the Lord your God with all your heart, and
with all your soul, and with all your strength, and with all
your mind; and your neighbour as yourself.

Luke 10.27

The Inner Journey

3
Learning to Pray

Pray as you can, not as you can't.

Dom Chapman

One of the disciples said to Jesus: 'Lord, teach us to pray,
as John taught his disciples.'

Luke 11.1

Why do we pray?

To be a Christian means to be in a close and growing relationship with God, Father, Son and Holy Spirit, a relationship the Bible dares to call a friendship. That friendship develops in part through worship, reading the Scriptures, fellowship with other Christians and through serving God and others but it develops also through personal prayer: time we spend with God on our own. Prayer is about far more than asking God for things on behalf of other people or ourselves: it is about building this relationship with God.

As we pray we are following the example of Jesus, whose pattern in the gospels is to set aside time regularly for solitary prayer. We are also following his teaching. In the Sermon on the Mount Jesus tells his followers to pray in secret:

> Whenever you pray, go into your own room and shut the door and pray to your Father who is in secret; and your Father who sees in secret will reward you.
>
> Matthew 6.6

As we pray, we strengthen and develop our relationship with God. We remember who we are before God. We re-orientate our lives, our desires and our will once again around God rather than ourselves.

Jesus gave the Lord's Prayer to his disciples as a pattern for prayer as well as words to learn and to use in prayer: it is a prayer which is meant to be prayed each day by a disciple of Christ ('Give us *this day* our daily bread'). Through the Lord's Prayer we learn to pray: 'Your will be done, on earth as it is in heaven' *before* we pray for our own needs.

Different Christians find different ways of praying helpful. Sometimes a person's pattern for prayer will be stable for long periods of their lives; sometimes there will be change and development as we change and develop as people. However long we have been Christians and however long we have been praying, we still have more to learn.

Establishing a foundation

For those who are new to faith, the most important thing is to begin to pray in the way which is most natural and helpful to you. If you can, work towards setting aside a time each day which is a regular time for prayer. It's better to begin with a short time and grow from there than to aim for too much too soon. Experiment with prayer at different times of the day. For most people, the very beginning of the day or the very end work best. For some, finding even five minutes when you are undisturbed can be very difficult, although it's still important to try.

Praying at the same time each day and in the same place is helpful to most people so that our prayer becomes a regular routine, just like our meals. Good habits can be as hard to establish as bad habits are to overcome so be prepared to keep going. Aim for a healthy discipline, in which you can be flexible without feeling guilty if you miss a prayer time. A place in the house where you can be on your own is easy for some people and hard for others. You may have a church nearby which is open for prayer; or you may be able to make a corner of your room into a prayer place with, perhaps, a candle or icon and a Bible and prayer book ready to hand. Our bodies are important: for most people sitting or kneeling will be the most natural posture. You need to be comfortable – but not too relaxed, especially if you pray last thing at night.

Most of us find it helpful to give a basic shape to our prayers which contains a balance of different elements and also to use at least some words written by other Christians or from the Scriptures. At the back of this book you will find a suggested outline for daily prayer for either the morning or the evening. It follows a basic structure: a time of preparation, reading the Bible, reflection upon the readings and prayers.

Praying at a set time each day doesn't mean, of course, that this is the only time when we might pray. Practising the presence of God at other times in the day can be extremely helpful. So can short prayers in difficult or dangerous situations; before meals; when the telephone rings or the doorbell goes or when the unexpected happens.

Find the natural rhythms of your day and develop a life of prayer which goes with the grain of your routine.

Learning to listen

Prayer is about listening to God as much as talking to him – or at least it should be. We listen as we read the Bible and reflect on what we read. We listen and try to discern God's voice as we write down our thoughts and reflections. We listen in the quietness of our own hearts to that still, small voice speaking within us: to affirm us; to call us; to guide us.

There are many different ways of listening to God. Through the years the Church has developed sensible and much needed guidelines for discerning when a Christian may be genuinely hearing God and when he or she may be hearing either simply their own desires or temptations from outside. These are some of the most important of these guidelines:

How do we recognize God's voice?

1. *Is what you have heard consistent with the Scriptures?* If it is, then it may be from God. If it isn't, then you should discard it.

2. *Does what you have heard lead to an increase of faith, hope or love in yourself or in other people?* If the answer is yes, this may be God's word to you.

3. *Does what you have heard draw you towards God or away from him?*

4. *If God is saying something to you for someone else, is that word for their upbuilding, encouragement or consolation* (1 Corinthians 14.3)? If it is not, then you have no right to share it.

5. *Is what you have heard consistent with what you believe God has said to you on earlier occasions?*

6. *Are you willing to subject what has been said to the discernment of other Christians?*

Emotions in prayer

Our emotions and feelings are part of being human and therefore part of our life of prayer and our wider relationship with God. Most Christians find that there are at least some periods in their life when they are aware of God's presence in terms of how they feel: people experience a sense of inner peace, of warmth, of joy or of security. These times are a gift from God and are to be appreciated and enjoyed. Many also find that at least some of the time God seems very distant or far away and prayer becomes dry routine and, occasionally, very difficult. There may be an obvious reason (such as an emotional turmoil in our lives like falling in love, bereavement or moving house) but sometimes there is no obvious cause that we can see. The wise counsel of Christians down the centuries has been that in these dry and difficult times when there are no obvious signs of God's presence it remains very important to keep going and to maintain our basic rhythms of prayer and worship. God is teaching us new lessons in faith, trust and perseverance. However, if such times persist, it may be the right time to talk with a trusted Christian friend or minister.

Answers to prayer

The Bible encourages us to pray for many different situations: for governments and those in authority; for the kingdom of God to be realized on earth; for those who are sick or in trouble; for Christian ministers and for the worldwide church; and for those who are our enemies or who we do not naturally like or get on with.

In many of these situations we are joining our prayers with those of the Church around the world for particular situations: we may not be able to see instant answers to prayer in what are often enormous situations of need. Our prayer is made in obedience and trust that somehow prayer which is sincerely offered will make a difference.

In situations closer to us, we should expect, often, to see prayer make a difference in the lives of those around us and in our own lives. The answers to prayer may seem to others to be nothing more than coincidence – it's just that when we don't pray the coincidences stop

happening! It is good to share the answers to prayer with other
Christians to build up our own faith and strengthen that of others.

However, not every prayer we pray will be answered. Praying is not
like wishing with a magic lamp. Sometimes we will need to think
again about what we are praying for. 'God, help me to win the
lottery'; 'God, I know he's married but please let him ask me out for a
drink'; 'God, let the Inland Revenue overlook my affairs this year' are
prayers we need to think hard about not praying. Sometimes though,
good and sincere prayers we pray for those we love or for ourselves
are not answered: people we care about suffer dreadfully or else they
die and God seems to do nothing.

At those times, which we all experience, we will be angry with God;
we will want to ask him very hard questions indeed, especially the
question 'why?'. As with any close friend, it is much better to be
honest than to be polite. The Book of Psalms in the Bible is full of
prayers which express every human emotion in prayer to God: anger,
hatred of others, jealousy, loneliness and deep hurt and sorrow. These
emotions may not all be 'correct', but if they are part of the way we
feel we need to be able to put them into words to God and
sometimes talk them through with others.

Finally, at other times, we may be the answer to our own prayers.
What use is it praying to God for the welfare of our parents or
children and then neglecting them ourselves? Or praying for the
relief of poverty and not being prepared to work, to give or to shop
in such a way that the poor are given practical help? Or to pray for
someone to lead the youth group at the church and not be
prepared to ask whether God may be calling you?

Going further and deeper

There are many books and guides to take you further into the
different ways of prayer. Your own church may have courses on offer.
The rhythm of the Church year gives opportunity for a deepening of
the life of prayer, especially in Lent and Advent (the seasons of the
year which come before Easter and Christmas). Many Christians are
helped through occasional quiet days or residential retreats of
different kinds. It can be helpful to talk through your life of prayer

from time to time with your minister or someone who acts as a spiritual guide or director. You may be helped by meeting to pray regularly with one or two others either in a shared form of prayer or in your own words. There are many different ways forward. The important thing is to keep moving on and to keep growing in this most important of relationships with Almighty God, Father, Son and Holy Spirit.

Readings and prayers

O Lord, my heart is not lifted up,
my eyes are not raised too high,
I do not occupy myself with things
too great and too marvellous for me.
But I have calmed and quieted my soul,
like a weaned child with its mother;
my soul is like the weaned child that is with me.

Psalm 131

Be still and know that I am God.

Psalm 46.10

A reflection on prayer

Your prayer will take countless forms
because it is the echo of your life,
and a reflection of the inexhaustible light
in which God dwells.

Sometimes you will taste and see how good the Lord is.
Be glad then, and give Him all honour,
because His goodness to you has no measure.
Sometimes you will be dry and joyless
like a parched land or an empty well.
But your thirst and helplessness

will be your best prayer
if you accept them with patience
and embrace them lovingly.
Sometimes your prayer will be an experience
of the infinite distance that separates you from God;
sometimes your being and His fullness
will flow into each other.
Sometimes you will be able to pray
only with your body and eyes;
sometimes your prayer will move beyond words
and images;
sometimes you will be able to leave everything
behind you
to concentrate on God and His Word.
Sometimes you will be able to do nothing else
but take your whole life and everything in you
and bring them before God.
Every hour has its own possibilities
of genuine prayer.

So set yourself again and again
on the way of prayer.

Rule for a New Brother

A prayer to repeat over and over, like breathing . . .

Lord Jesus Christ, Son of the living God, have mercy
on me, a sinner.

Lord, make me an instrument of your peace;
where there is hatred, let me sow love,
where there is injury, let me sow pardon,
where there is doubt, let me sow faith,
where there is despair, let me give hope,
where there is darkness, let me give light,
where there is sadness, let me give joy.

O divine master, grant that I may
not try to be comforted but to comfort
not try to be understood but to understand
not try to be loved, but to love.
Because it is in giving that we are received,
it is in forgiving that we are forgiven,
and it is in dying that we are born to eternal life.

Ascribed to St Francis of Assisi

Thanks be to you,
my Lord Jesus Christ,
for all the blessings and benefits
which you have given to me,
for all the pains and insults
you have borne for me.
O most merciful Friend
my Brother and Redeemer,
may I know you more clearly,
love you more dearly
and follow you more nearly
day by day.

St Richard of Chichester

Christ be with me, Christ within me,
Christ behind me, Christ before me,
Christ beside me, Christ to win me,
Christ to comfort and restore me,
Christ beneath me, Christ above me,
Christ in quiet, Christ in danger,
Christ in hearts of all that love me,
Christ in mouth of friend and stranger.

St Patrick's Breastplate

Go before us, Lord, in all we do
with your most gracious favour,
and guide us with your continual help,
that in all our works
begun, continued and ended in you,
we may glorify your holy name,
and finally by your mercy receive everlasting life;
through Jesus Christ our Lord.

The Christian Year: Collects and Post Communion Prayers for
Sundays and Festivals (Fourth Sunday Before Lent)

God be in my head and in my understanding
God be in my eyes and in my looking
God be in my mouth and in my speaking
God be in my heart and in my thinking
God be at my end and at my departing.

The Sarum Primer

Be thou a bright flame before me,
Be thou a guiding star above me,
Be thou a smooth path below me,
Be thou a kindly shepherd behind me,
Today – tonight – and forever.

St Columba of Iona

A General Thanksgiving

Almighty God, Father of all mercies,
we your unworthy servants give you most
    humble and hearty thanks
for all your goodness and loving kindness
to us and to all people.
We bless you for our creation, preservation
    and all the blessings of this life;
but above all for your immeasurable love
in the redemption of the world by our Lord Jesus Christ,

for the means of grace, and for the hope of glory.
And give us, we pray, such a sense of all your mercies
that our hearts may be unfeignedly thankful,
and that we show forth your praise,
not only with our lips but in our lives,
by giving up ourselves to your service,
and by walking before you in holiness
   and righteousness all our days;
through Jesus Christ our Lord,
to whom, with you and the Holy Spirit
   be all honour and glory
for ever and ever. Amen.

Common Worship: Daily Prayer

Prayer

Prayer the Church's banquet, Angel's age,
   God's breath in man returning to his birth,
   The soul in paraphrase, heart in pilgrimage,
The Christian plummet, sounding heaven and earth;
Engine against th'Almighty, sinners' tower,
   Reversed thunder, Christ-side-piercing spear,
   The six-days world transposing in an hour,
A kind of tune, which all things hear and fear;
Softness, and peace, and joy, and love, and bliss,
   Exalted Manna, gladness of the best,
   Heaven in ordinary, man well drest,
The milky way, the bird of Paradise,
   Church-bells beyond the stars heard,
   the souls blood
   The land of spices; something understood.

George Herbert

4
Exploring the Scriptures

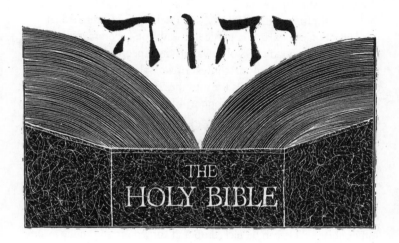

Your word is a lamp to my feet and a light to my path.

Psalm 119.105

Blessed Lord,
who caused all holy Scriptures
   to be written for our learning:
help us so to hear them,
to read, mark, learn and inwardly digest them
that, through patience, and the comfort of your
   holy word,
we may embrace and for ever hold fast
   the hope of everlasting life,
which you have given us in our Saviour Jesus Christ.

The Christian Year: Collects and Post Communion Prayers for
Sundays and Festivals (Last Sunday After Trinity)

The Bible is a unique book in the history of the world, not simply a special book for Christians. The books Christians call the Old Testament are the foundation writings of the Jewish faith and both Old and New Testaments are regarded as sacred in Islam. Through these three world faiths, the Scriptures have come to shape (and still shape) many aspects of world history and culture.

For individual Christians and for the Church, the Bible holds a unique place. The testimony of the Bible itself, affirmed by the Church, is that the Scriptures are inspired by God (literally 'God-breathed'). In this collection of books, in a particular way, God is communicating his love and the good news of salvation to all people for all time. As the Bible is read today in the context of worship and prayerful study, God continues to breathe his life into the Scriptures for the building up, challenging, teaching and comfort of the Christian community.

The Bible is part of our heritage as Christians. It is also a rich and essential resource for our own journey with Christ. As Christians we need to know something about the Bible and to begin to explore its treasures, both on our own and with others.

A library of different books

Although the Bible can be picked up and carried around today as one book, it is much more like a library than a single volume. Just as you will find different kinds of books in your public library, so you will find different kinds of books in the Bible. You may never have thought about it, but we read different kinds of books in different ways. With a novel or a history book we start on the first page and expect to be able to read to the end following the story and being entertained and interested along the way. We wouldn't dream of doing the same thing with an encyclopaedia; a cookery book; or a guide to our legal system. We need to approach the books of the Bible in a similar way: we will find a common thread and story running through the whole – but we should read the different volumes in different ways.

Open your Bible at the 'contents' page. You will find 39 books in the Old Testament section of the library. They were written over a period of more than a 1,000 years and tell the story of the nation of Israel from the time of Abraham (around 1,800 years before Christ) to the time of Ezra (around 400 years before Christ). Somewhere in the front of many English Bibles you will find a time chart or time line showing the main divisions of the history of Israel and some maps giving you some idea of the geography. The Old Testament books were written in Hebrew (with a little Aramaic). As well as the history of the people of Israel, the books contain their laws; their sacred hymns and songs; wise sayings; stories and parables and a great many of the writings of Israel's prophets. From a Christian perspective, the books of the Old Testament look forward to the coming of Christ and prepare the way for him.

In the New Testament section you will find 26 books, although many of them are very short. The New Testament was written over a much shorter period of time (around 50 years) and was written in Greek, the common language of the Roman Empire. The two main types of books are the gospels and the letters. The gospels were written to tell us the story of Jesus: not his life story (there is very little about anything but the final three years) but the story of his ministry and teaching, death and resurrection. The letters were mainly written to groups of Christians scattered around the ancient world to teach and guide them in the Christian way. The Book of Acts tells the story of the early church and the Book of Revelation, right at the end of the New Testament, was written to help Christians in every generation to see the spiritual truths and realities behind the often disturbing events in the world and human society.

The Early Church inherited the collection of Old Testament books from the Jewish people. You will find in some English Bibles another series of books bound between the Old and New Testaments called the Apocrypha (or deutero-canonical books). These are books which were not part of the Jewish scriptures but were still held to be special and useful in some way and they have been regarded in the same light by much of the Christian Church.

Choosing a Bible

Take care when reading the Bible to choose a good, modern English translation. Bibles which have been passed down within the family or given as confirmation presents are often the old versions: good to dip into but not helpful for most people's everyday use. Choose a Bible which will last a good while and which is easy to carry if you are going to take it to meetings or to church. You may want one which includes help to understand the text, introductions to the different books or a reading plan. Make sure the Bible you use regularly is a translation of the Biblical languages – that is a faithful rendering of what is there in the original text – and not a paraphrase (putting into English what people think the text means). Ask someone in your church or a Christian bookshop for help if you have any questions.

Is the Bible without error?

All Christians believe that the Scriptures are inspired by God and authoritative in matters of Christian faith and practice. Some Christians go further and believe and argue that the Bible is completely without error in terms of historical and scientific fact. This claim has never been made in the creeds of the Church or in the foundation articles and documents of the Church of England. You will find as you read and study the Bible that, as well as being 'God-breathed', the Bible is a very human book. Different authors and groups exposed their own cultural assumptions and particular points of view in the different strands in the Scriptures. There are places where different parts of the Scriptures reflect different perspectives. Parts of the Old Testament in particular are completed or superseded by what comes later, most of all in Christ. Parts of the Scriptures are not and do not claim to be historically or scientifically accurate in every detail: they have a different purpose and message.

The truth that God was and is at work in these ancient and very human texts should come as no surprise to Christian people. At the centre of the Christian faith is the claim that almighty God became a human being and transformed our humanity. We believe that in the service of Holy Communion, God is at work and present through faith in bread and wine made by men and women. In the Church, too, God is present and at work, by his grace, although that Church is all too human and imperfect. So through the Scriptures, Christians believe that God has spoken and still speaks his life-giving word into human lives in a particular and unique way. The only way to test that claim is to trust it and experience God's word through the Bible for yourself.

Where do I begin?

If you don't know the Bible well and would like to begin to explore its pages there are two things you need to avoid. Don't be tempted to use it like a lucky dip, just opening the pages at random each day and reading what you find. Don't try and work your way through it beginning at Genesis and aiming for Revelation. Most people who do that give up when they reach the second half of Exodus. Many Bibles contain simple reading plans to help those who don't know the Scriptures very well.

Reading with a lectionary

The Bible readings in your church on Sundays will almost certainly be guided by a lectionary: a table of readings agreed by the Church centrally. A good way to link your own Bible reading with the readings and sermons you will hear on Sundays is to read each Sunday's lessons again in the week following and reflect upon them. The Church of England also publishes a lectionary with set psalms, Old Testament and New Testament readings for Morning and Evening Prayer. Following these will take you through much of the Bible over a two-year period.

Using Bible-reading notes

Several Christian publishers produce Bible-reading notes to help Christians in their personal Bible reading. Again these can be used as part of your daily time of prayer. Some are undated and follow particular themes. Others give a set passage for each day and are produced quarterly.

With a partner

If you are not used to reading the Bible you will probably have at least some questions about what you are reading. It can be helpful in the early years of your Christian life to study the Bible with someone else who has been a Christian for a little longer. Simply agree to meet once a month for this purpose. Agree in advance what you will read together. Write down any comments or questions on passages whilst you are reading on your own and then go through them together.

In a small group

Many churches or groups of churches have small groups where studying Scripture together plays a central role. You will find you learn more from engaging with the Bible if this is done in the context of a group of other Christians seeking to learn from, and to put into practice, the different things they read.

Ways of listening to God through the Scriptures

Reflective reading (with notes)

● Ask God to speak to you through his word.

● Read the set passage slowly and carefully. If you are using notes read the notes as well to start you thinking.

● Ask some simple questions of the passage. What do I learn about God? About myself? About the Christian life?

● Give some space to attending to God and reflecting on what he says to you.

● Move from here into other parts of your prayers.

Meditation on one verse

● Choose a suitable verse.

● Prepare to pray. Take some time to be still.

● Repeat the verse slowly to yourself for several minutes until it begins to become part of you. Think of it in context. If it's a prayer, address it to the Lord. If the words are from God, imagine him speaking them to your heart and life.

● Take the first word or phrase. Turn the word over in your mind. Think about what it means. Give God space to speak to you.

● When you come to the end of that word or phrase (after minutes or days), go on to the next. As God begins to speak to you follow his lead – not your method.

Imaginative contemplation

This way of listening is especially helpful with passages from the gospels.

● Choose the passage before your prayer time – preferably the day before – and read it through several times.

● Take some time to be still and remember all God's love for you.

● Set the scene for the passage in your imagination. Picture the place. Use your senses imaginatively. What can you see, hear, smell, taste and feel?

● Set the people in the scene. How do they feel about each other? Where are you and whose side are you on?

● 'Play' the scene in your imagination as slowly as you can. Listen carefully especially to any words spoken by Jesus or to Jesus. Listen to your own feelings – especially towards Jesus.

● Meet Jesus on your own after the whole scene has been played through. Listen to what he is saying to you. Share your own feelings with him.

Readings and prayers

All scripture is inspired by God and is useful for
teaching, for reproof, for correction and for training
in righteousness.

2 Timothy 3.16

Holy Scripture containeth all things necessary to
salvation: so that whatsoever is not read therein, nor
may be proved thereby, is not to be required of any
man, that it should be believed as an article of
the Faith, or be thought requisite or necessary to
salvation. In the name of the holy Scripture we do
understand those Canonical Books of the Old and New
Testament, of whose authority was never in any doubt
in the Church.

The Book of Common Prayer,
Article VI of the Articles of Religion

The word of God is living and active, sharper than any
two-edged sword, piercing until it divides soul from
spirit, joints from marrow; it is able to judge the
thoughts and intentions of the heart.

Hebrews 4.12

Lord God,
you feed us with the living bread from heaven;
you renew our faith,
increase our hope,
and strengthen our love.
Teach us to hunger
for Christ who is the true and living bread,
and to live by every word
that comes from your mouth,
through Jesus Christ our Lord.

New Patterns for Worship

The word of God should lead us first of all to
contemplation and meditation. Instead of taking the
words apart, we should bring them together in our
innermost being; instead of wondering if we agree or
disagree, we should wonder which words are directly
spoken to us and connect directly with our most
personal story. Instead of thinking about the words as
potential subjects for an interesting dialogue or paper,
we should be willing to let them penetrate into the most
hidden corners of our heart, even to those places where
no other word has yet found entrance. Then and only
then can the word bear fruit as seed sown in rich soil.
Only then can we 'hear and understand' (Matthew 13.23)

Henri Nouwen, *Reaching Out*

A Song of the Word

Seek the Lord while he may be found:
call on him while he is near.
Let the wicked abandon their ways:
and the unrighteous their thoughts.
Turn back to the Lord, who will have mercy:
to our God, who will richly pardon.
'For my thoughts are not your thoughts:
neither are your ways my ways', says the Lord.
'As the heavens are higher than the earth:
so are my ways higher than your ways
and my thoughts higher than your thoughts.
As the rain and snow come down from heaven:
and return not again but water the earth,
bringing forth life and giving growth:
seed for sowing and bread to eat,
so is my word that goes out from my mouth:
it does not return to me empty,
but it will accomplish my purpose:
and succeed in the task I give it'.

Isaiah 55.6-11, from *Patterns for Worship*

45

Most people are bothered by those passages in
Scripture which they cannot understand; but as for
me, I always notice that the passages in Scripture
which trouble me most are those that I do understand.

Mark Twain

Break thou the bread of life,
dear Lord, to me,
as thou didst break the loaves
beside the sea;
beyond the sacred page
I seek thee, Lord,
my spirit longs for thee,
O living Word.

Bless thou the truth, dear Lord,
to me, to me
as thou didst bless the bread
by Galilee;
then shall all bondage cease,
all fetters fall,
and I shall find my peace,
my all in all.

Mary A. Lathbury, *Break Thou the Bread of Life*

5
Food for the Journey

The great thing to remember about a sacrament
is this: that God always turns up.

Richard Giles

Anyone who eats this bread will live forever.

John 6.58

On the night before he died Jesus shared a meal with his friends. His words at this meal are mysterious and wonderful. As he broke some bread he said it was his body. As he shared wine he said it was his blood. He then said that this should always be done when Christians meet together in remembrance of him.

A parable of grace

Down through the centuries Christian people have been faithful to this last command of Jesus. We give the service many different names – the Eucharist, Mass, Holy Communion – but in all denominations and traditions what we are doing is essentially the same: we take, bless and share bread and wine in remembrance of the passion, death and resurrection of Jesus. For the actions of the Christian Eucharist – bread broken, wine poured out – not only vividly recall the way Jesus died, they also show how we are called to be eucharistic people. Today God wants to take us and bless us, even in our brokenness, in order that our lives may be used to his glory.

In this sense the Eucharist is like an acted parable. It helps us understand the meaning of Jesus' death and of how God calls us to sacrificial living. Among all the different words we use to describe the service, Eucharist is probably the best. It means 'thank you'.

A sacrament of love

The Eucharist is also what the Church calls a sacrament or sign of God's love. A sacrament is defined in *The Book of Common Prayer* as 'an outward and visible sign of an inward and spiritual grace'. Holy Communion and Baptism are the two great sacraments of the Christian Church, instituted by Christ himself.

There are also five other sacramental ministries of grace recognized by many Christians: confirmation, ordination, marriage, reconciliation and healing.

They have developed in the life of the church to meet different needs, but all of them have their origin in Jesus' own ministry and in the apostolic life. Their purpose is strength for the journey of the Christian life. Confirmation is about being strengthened through the gift of the Holy Spirit. Marriage and ordination obviously refer to specific vocations that God calls us to as we travel through life. Reconciliation and healing are for making peace with God: forgiveness after we have confessed our sin; and healing where there is brokeness in body, mind or spirit.

Many churches always have a Eucharist as their main service on a Sunday. Some churches celebrate the Eucharist every day.

At the centre of the Eucharist is receiving Jesus in the sacrament. 'The bread that we break,' says Paul, 'is it not a sharing in the body of Christ?' (1 Corinthians 10.16).

Through the power of the Holy Spirit, and the prayer of the Christian assembly, the bread and wine of the Eucharist by faith take on a new value so that in receiving the bread and the wine we receive Jesus: the Jesus who promised he would always be with us. (Matthew 28.20). We affirm, and reverently experience, that when Jesus said 'This is my body, this is my blood, do this to remember me', he meant it. His risen life, the life he won for us on the cross, is communicated by the taking, breaking and sharing of bread and wine.

It is impossible to understand or to grasp exactly how Jesus is present when we receive the bread and the wine. Over the centuries, the Church has wrestled with these different understandings and Christians have often been divided over something which should unite us. How Jesus comes to us is indeed a mystery, but his presence is more than symbolic. When I hold out my hands to receive the bread of the Eucharist I dare to believe that I am receiving the risen life of Jesus who loves me and who died for me. Therefore

I approach the table of the Lord with reverence, thanksgiving and expectation. It is the place where, more than anywhere else, I can receive what I need to live the Christian life. It is the place where Jesus feeds me with his life. The bread of eternal life is made available on earth.

I need, therefore, to prepare myself for receiving Holy Communion. It is always good to say prayers of preparation: it has been a tradition for some Christians to refrain from eating for an hour before receiving communion as a small, but very tangible, sign of our preferring nothing to Christ. I also need to be thankful afterwards, thinking how I can show Christ to others in my daily life and live the life I have received. As well as uniting us with Christ, Holy Communion also unites us with one another: 'Because there is one bread, we who are many are one body, for we all partake of the one bread' (1 Corinthians 10.17).

To safeguard the unity of the Eucharist and of the Christian community, and to stop it becoming a private affair between me and God, in the Church of England, as with most other churches, only an ordained priest can preside at the Eucharist. This is also the reason why the Church of England holds it important for an authorized Eucharistic Prayer to be used. These prayers express the faith of the church down through the centuries, uniting us not only with one another but with Christian people who have gone before us.

Backwards and forwards

The Eucharist is not only a meal for the present. As we gather together around the Lord's table we look backwards into history and we tell again the story of our creation and salvation. The Last Supper itself was a Passover meal and so we remember in Christian worship the way in which God saved his ancient people from slavery in Egypt for freedom in the promised land. We remember the meals Jesus shared with his disciples, especially in the Upper Room. Most of all we are remembering Jesus' death on the cross for our sins: his once and for all perfect and complete sacrifice for the sins of the whole world. In the words of the great prayer of thanksgiving:

He opened wide his arms for us on the cross;
he put an end to death by dying for us;
and revealed the resurrection by rising to new life;
so he fulfilled your will and won for you a holy people.

Common Worship: Holy Communion
(Eucharistic Prayer B)

As we look back at our common history, so we look forward together. One of the greatest pictures of heaven in the Bible is the picture of the great banquet in heaven. In the Eucharist, our own worship is joined with the worship of heaven now: 'with angels and archangels and with all the company of heaven'. We look forward together to the time when Christ will return and we shall be gathered together with him for ever:

Send the Holy Spirit on your people
and gather into one in your kingdom
all who share this one bread and one cup,
so that we, in the company of all the saints,
may praise and glorify you for ever,
through Jesus Christ our Lord.

Common Worship: Holy Communion
(Eucharistic Prayer B)

The shape of the service

It is best to think of the Eucharist as three encounters:

- in the living bread of Holy Communion;
- in the living word of holy Scripture;
- in the living body of a holy people.

And as a great commissioning sent out to love and work to God's praise and glory!

The basic shape and ceremony of the Eucharist is governed by these encounters, enabling us to receive Christ in order to serve him in the world.

First of all we gather as God's holy people. We sing a hymn of praise and we acknowledge our need of God, usually with set prayers, often prayers of confession and absolution.

Then the service falls into two main parts. In the liturgy of the word the Scriptures are broken open in order to be received and understood: there are readings, an address, prayers and often we recite the creed. In the liturgy of the sacrament the bread and wine are taken, blessed, broken and shared. The word 'liturgy' means literally 'the work of the people'. It describes the fact that Christian worship is not a spectator sport, but a participative drama. We all have a part to play and more and more the church is wanting to find ways of expressing everyone's gifts within the liturgy. However, often today we think of the word 'liturgy' as just meaning the words of the service on the pages of a book. We do have set prayers, and these are valuable and important, but Christian worship calls for much more – the offering of our whole selves to God, all our gifts and insights in a great sacrifice of praise.

In the Church of England, at the pivotal point between encountering Jesus in his word and in the sacrament we turn to each other and exchange a sign of peace. This too is an encounter with Jesus. We greet the person of Jesus in the face of our neighbour. We belong to one another. This Holy Communion is sealed by sharing bread and wine. We become what we eat – the body of Christ.

In all of these ways we encounter Christ in the Eucharist: in the words of Scripture, in one another and in the bread and wine. At the end of the service, as the last part of the great drama, we dedicate ourselves in God's service. We are sent out in mission: 'Go in peace,' says the service leader, 'to love and serve the Lord.' We come together to be sent out.

Sunday worship

I am not a Christian by myself. I am part of the body of Christ. Sunday is the Lord's day, the day of Resurrection and the day when the Christian community gathers to praise God. I am defined by my worship. Here I am most fully myself, for here I am most fully in communion with God and with my fellow human beings. Here I renew my commitment to Christ and I receive the resources and energy I need to live as a disciple of Jesus. The life of worship, and the particular sustenance of the sacraments, are both rations for my Christian journey, and a foretaste of the glory that awaits me in heaven.

For these reasons I must be faithful in worship and every Christian should make every effort to participate in the worship of the church on Sunday. Where other commitments, especially work, make this impossible we must either look for other opportunities to join the Christian household at prayer during the week, or else make sure we make what is called a spiritual communion. This is simply setting aside time on Sunday to unite ourselves with the praises being offered by the church and ask Jesus to come and make his home with us. Below are some prayers we could use for this.

Finally worship means giving honour. Not only am I most completely myself when I worship, but also it is in worship, that I most completely (in this life!) face up to the reality of God in all his majesty and all his mercy. If I want to travel through life as a Christian, it is worship that will make this possible.

Many people outside the Church think of worship as a flight from reality. They couldn't be more wrong. There is nothing more real. Worship is the only thing I am doing on earth that I am sure I will still be doing in heaven!

Readings and prayers

For I received from the Lord what I also handed on to you, that the Lord Jesus on the night when he was betrayed took a loaf of bread, and when he had given thanks, he broke it and said, 'This is my body that is given for you. Do this in remembrance of me.' In the same way he took the cup also after supper, saying, 'This cup is the new covenant in my blood. Whenever you drink it, do this as a memorial of me.' Whenever you eat this bread, then, and drink this cup, you are proclaiming the Lord's death until he comes.

1 Corinthians 11.23-26

Prayers of preparation for receiving Holy Communion

Almighty God,
to whom all hearts are open,
all desires known,
and from whom no secrets are hidden:
cleanse the thoughts of our hearts
by the inspiration of your Holy Spirit,
that we may perfectly love you,
and worthily magnify your holy name;
through Christ our Lord.
Amen.

Common Worship: Holy Communion (Prayer of Preparation)

We do not presume
to come to this your table, merciful Lord,
trusting in our own righteousness,
but in your manifold and great mercies.
We are not worthy
so much as to gather up the crumbs under your table.
But you are the same Lord
whose nature is always to have mercy.
Grant us, therefore, gracious Lord,

so to eat the flesh of your dear Son Jesus Christ
and to drink his blood,
that our sinful bodies may be made clean by his body
and our souls washed through his most precious blood
that we may evermore dwell in him, and he in us.
Amen.

Common Worship: Holy Communion (Giving of Communion)

Almighty and ever living God,
I approach the sacrament of your only-begotten Son,
Our Lord Jesus Christ
I come sick to the doctor of life,
Unclean to the fountain of mercy,
Blind to the radiance of eternal light,
And poor and needy to the Lord of heaven and earth.
Lord, in your great generosity,
Heal my sickness, wash away my defilement,
Enlighten my blindness, enrich my poverty,
And clothe my nakedness.
May I receive the bread of angels,
The King of kings and Lord of lords,
With humble reverence
With the purity and faith,
The repentance and love, and the determined purpose
That will bring me to salvation.
May I receive the sacrament of the Lord's body
and blood,
And its reality and power.
In God
May I receive the body of your only-begotten Son,
our Lord Jesus Christ,
Born from the womb of the Virgin Mary,
And so be received into his mystical body,
And numbered among his members.
Loving Father,
As on my earthly pilgrimage
I now receive your beloved Son

Under the veil of a sacrament,
May I one day see him face to face in glory,
Who lives and reigns with you for ever. Amen.

St Thomas Aquinas

Prayers of thanksgiving after Holy Communion

Almighty God,
we thank you for feeding us
with the body and blood of your Son Jesus Christ.
Through him we offer you our souls and bodies
to be a living sacrifice.
Send us out
in the power of your Spirit
to live and work
to your praise and glory.
Amen.

Common Worship: Holy Communion
(Prayer after Communion)

Father of all,
we give you thanks and praise,
that when we were still far off
you met us in your Son and brought us home.
Dying and living, he declared your love,
gave us grace, and opened the gate of glory.
May we who share Christ's body live his risen life;
we who drink his cup bring life to others;
we whom the Spirit lights give light to the world.
Keep us firm in the hope you have set before us,
so we and all your children shall be free,
and the whole earth live to praise your name;
through Jesus Christ our Lord.
Amen.

Common Worship: Holy Communion
(Prayer after Communion)

Walk with us, Lord,
along the road of resurrection!

Explain for us, so slow to believe,
the things that Scripture says of you.
Break the Bread of the Eucharist with us
Whenever we share our lives with our brothers and sisters.

Stay with us
Each time night approaches
And the daylight fades in our hearts!

Lucien Deiss, Come Lord Jesus

For reflection on Holy Communion

Our Lord Jesus said:
I am the bread of life. Whoever comes to me shall
never be hungry, and whoever believes in me shall never
be thirsty.
I am the living bread which has come down from
heaven: if anyone eats this bread he shall live for ever.
Moreover, the bread which I shall give is my own flesh;
I give it for the life of the world.
My flesh is real food; my blood is real drink. Whoever
eats my flesh and drinks my blood dwells continually
in me and I dwell in him.

The apostle Paul wrote:
The cup of blessing which we bless,
is it not a participation in the blood of Christ?
The bread which we break,
is it not a participation in the body of Christ?
Because there is one loaf, we who are many are one body,
for we all partake of the same loaf.
As often as you eat this bread and drink the cup,
you proclaim the Lord's death until he comes.
Whoever therefore eats the bread or drinks the cup
of the Lord in an unworthy manner

will be guilty of profaning the body and blood
of the Lord.
Let us examine ourselves,
and so eat of the bread and drink of the cup.
Let us reflect how in Holy Communion
the night of Christ's birth
the night in which he was betrayed,
the hours on the cross,
the morning of resurrection, the glory of the ascension,
and our own worship and need
are brought together in one eternal moment.
Let us thank God that throughout the world
the Holy Communion is the most loved
and solemn act of Christian worship;
that in this sacrament Christ comes to us
in forgiveness and love,
to unite us to himself
to transform us for his service.

Frank Colquhoun

Life drawn from the Eucharist makes all kinds of demands
on you to proclaim the meaning and greatness of this
mystery. You are called especially to give the sacrament
its full effect in unity, brotherhood and service. The unity
of all Christians and all people must be closest to your
heart. always and everywhere you are called to rise above
oppositions and divisions in the universal love of Christ.
Always look for what unites and fight everything that
estranges and separates people from each other.

The Eucharist sets you on the way of Christ. It takes you
into his redeeming death and gives you a share in the most
radical deliverance possible. And already the light of the
resurrection, the new creation, is streaming through it
from beyond. Whenever you sit at table with the risen Lord,
it is the first day of the week, very early in the morning.

Rule for a New Brother

6
Travelling Together

The church is never a place, but always a people; never
a fold, but always a flock; never a sacred building, but
always a believing assembly. The church is you who
pray, not where you pray. A structure of brick and
marble can no more be a church than your clothes
of serge or satin can be you.

Anon

We, who are many, are one body in Christ, and
individually we are members one of another.

Romans 12.5

You cannot be a Christian by yourself. Christ has come to break down barriers of separation. Although some people insist it is possible to be a Christian without going to church this is a dangerous folly since it can so easily lead to isolation and individualism. It is probably propagated by the mistaken belief that being a Christian equals 'being good', and, of course, it is possible to be 'good' (as our society understands it) without going to church. But the Church is not made up of people who think they are better than others, but of people who want to be better than they are. And part of that 'being better' is about our responsibilities and commitments to each other. Once we have made the most basic Christian declaration that God is 'Our Father', then we are inextricably linked to each other. We have no choice but to leave individualism behind.

The Church of Jesus Christ is a new communion, binding human beings in relationship with one another and with God. Paul describes this relationship as being like a Body, with Christ at the head (see 1 Corinthians 12). As we shall see this image also explains and encourages the interdependence of different gifts and ministries within the Church. Just as the different parts of the body work together supporting and complementing one another, so it is within the Church.

In other words we cannot think of the Church as an external reality. We are the Church. We are Christ. We are part of a new humanity. We are the people of God.

Of course it doesn't always feel like this. Sometimes the experience of attending a church on Sunday will be uninteresting, and the motley collection of human beings we encounter unfriendly. However this does not change the inner reality of this new network of relationships formed by our membership of the Church.

We should try to avoid the mistake of simply judging the Church by what our eyes see and ears hear. Because the Church is people, then it will, in its visible, external life, be fallible and compromised; but the Church is also Christ, and in its inner life is the channel for God's grace and truth. As we reminded ourselves right at the beginning of this book God is Holy Trinity – Father, Son and Holy Spirit. God is a community of persons in loving relationship. The

Christian faith offers an invitation for all humanity to join in this relationship, therefore the Church is reflecting and establishing the life of God. To cut ourselves off from the Church is to run the very serious risk of cutting ourselves off from Christ.

This is what Jesus himself says of the relationship in John's gospel:

> I am the vine,
> You are the branches.
> Those who abide in me and I in them bear much fruit,
> Because apart from me you can do nothing.
>
> John 15.5

The Church then is Holy Communion. And within the fellowship of the Church we enjoy certain privileges, and we must meet certain responsibilities.

Worship

At the centre of Church life, as we have seen, is the great rhythm of worship and mission. We come together to praise God, affirm our identity in Christ and to be built up and sustained in our Christian lives. We are sent out to share in the great mission of God to his world: loving others for God's sake. The greatest commandments are the command to love God and to love others.

Our love for God is expressed through our common worship as well as through our own prayers and our life together. The word 'worship' is from the Old English meaning 'to give worth' to something in our lives. For most Christians it is still possible to gather together on Sundays: we set aside the first part of the first day of the week for the worship of God with other Christians. In simply being there we are making a statement that we are putting God in the first place in our lives. In a society in which Sunday is becoming more and more like the other days of the week, Christians need to work harder to retain the importance of worship each and every Sunday. If we ourselves have to work on Sundays, that worship will need to be expressed at a different time of the week.

At the heart of worship for most Anglicans is Holy Communion. As we have already seen, the Eucharist both re-creates and sustains us as Christ's body here on earth. Therefore to encounter and receive Jesus in Holy Communion is both the greatest joy and the most solemn responsibility of the Christian life. How could we absent ourselves from his table once we have glimpsed just the tiniest hint of what is on offer? It is vital that personal faith in Jesus becomes corporate life in his church. Gathering together Sunday by Sunday is the surest sign of this communion with one another and with God.

One, Holy, Catholic and Apostolic

But the Church is more than just the local church. If it is the body of Christ then it has a life beyond the local and beyond the physical. In the creed we affirm belief in the one Church, 'holy, catholic and apostolic'. What do these words mean?

To say that the Church is *one* is to describe that essential unity, which lies at the heart of church membership. Although 2000 years of Christian history have brought sad and painful division, the Church, in her inner life, is one. We must strive to make that unity a visible reality.

To say that the Church is *holy* is to describe our relationship with God. God is holy and because we are in communion with God we become a holy people. The word 'holy' means, originally, 'set apart' for God and therefore in some ways different from society around us.

To say that the Church is *catholic* is to describe our relationship with one another. We are the community of believers, part of a universal Church stretching into every corner of the earth. But in the Apostles' Creed we also state our belief in the communion of saints. Hence we are also part of a communion which stretches beyond this earth and beyond the confines of this life. The word 'catholic' describes a quality of life that is forever yearning for wholeness and community. Some people mistakenly think catholic means Roman Catholic. But this cannot be: all of us are part of Christ's Catholic Church.

To say that the Church is *apostolic* is to describe both our relationship with the apostles themselves and with the world. 'Apostolic' means that we are built upon the foundations of those who went before us. The Church stretches back in history as well as forward into eternity. But the literal meaning of 'apostle' is 'one who is sent'. Jesus says to his disciples: 'As the Father has sent me, so I send you' (John 20.21). The apostolic Church is a Church sharing in God's searching love for the world, a Church longing to bring all humanity into new relationship with God. The apostolic Church is still a missionary Church.

Commitment

Part of belonging to the Church is sharing responsibility. Jesus entrusts his mission to us.

We must be one – striving for visible unity with other Christians and finding practical ways of working together with other churches. This will be for the good of our local community, but also because it is Christ's prayer for his Church.

We must be holy – faithful in public worship and in personal prayer and striving to be distinctive and faithful in our lifestyle.

We must maintain and build the catholicity of the Church. As well as taking part in the full life of the local church we must also be part of the wider Church. For Anglicans this means the diocese and the wider Anglican Communion (the fellowship of Anglican Churches which extends throughout the world).

The Anglican Church is a worldwide communion of churches. Every Anglican parish is part of a diocese led by a Bishop and together these dioceses make up the different provinces of the Anglican Church. In England there are two provinces (Canterbury and York), forty-two dioceses, and thousands of parishes covering every square inch of our country and providing ministry to every single person. In local areas groups of Anglican parishes are also linked together in what are called deaneries, and ecumenically in local groups known as 'Churches Together'. Increasingly some denominations are also sharing buildings and certain ministries in what are called local ecumenical partnerships.

We must also look for other, smaller, ways of celebrating and building up our unity with one another. In many churches, nowadays, membership of the church is expressed in a smaller house group or community as well as in a larger congregation. This can be a vital way of sustaining faith and harks back to the earliest life of the Church when meetings were probably in people's homes. It is useful to take every opportunity to be part of such a group if it is available in your church. It increases our sense of belonging, and often can provide the forum for learning about the faith, discovering our own gifts and ministries, and for service and mission together.

We must develop the apostolic life of the Church. Even though we travel together as the people of God, much of our living out of the Christian faith will be in daily life and separate from the immediate support of the church and even the presence of other Christians. It is at these times that it is easy to forget the gospel and to find our lives indistinguishable from others who do not share our faith. We will return to explore these themes in detail in the next part of the book, but for now we need to remember that the apostolic calling is given to us all, and according to our different passions, gifts and personalities each of us is called to represent Christ.

Within the life of a local church we need to develop local mission projects so that the church visibly expresses God's priorities. We also need to become missionary congregations – taking the agenda of our life from God's ongoing mission of love.

Joy

The joy of being part of Christ's Church is that we are never alone. We are part of something bigger than ourselves, we are surrounded and supported by the prayers of saints and angels, and we are in solidarity with Christian people throughout the world in many different cultures, traditions and denominations. We travel together. The events of our life – the joys of birth and marriage – the sorrows of pain and death – are marked and celebrated and given meaning. I rediscover my life as a pilgrimage home, and the company of believers – whether I happen to like them or not – as fellow travellers. This joy of travelling together is one of the very best parts of the Christian life.

Readings and prayers

If anyone is in Christ, there is a new creation:
everything old has passed away; see, everything has
become new! All this is from God, who reconciled us
to himself through Christ, and has given us the
ministry of reconciliation.

2 Corinthians 5.17-18

Heavenly Father,
you have called us
in the Body of your Son Jesus Christ
to continue his work of reconciliation
and to reveal you to all people.
Forgive us the sins which tear us apart,
give us courage to overcome our fears and to seek
unity
which is your gift and your will.
We ask this through Jesus Christ our Lord.

Look upon us, O Lord,
and grant us the grace of your Holy Spirit.
Where there is weakness, give us strength,
where there is disagreement, give us tolerance,
where there is misunderstanding, give us patience;
where there is hurt, give us courage to forgive
and the grace to accept forgiveness.
Be present in your church here and in all places;
bless our work, and everything that is undertaken
by our Christian sisters and brothers,
for the furtherance of your kingdom
of unity and love, peace and justice.

Uniting Prayer, compiled by the
West Yorkshire Ecumenical Council

Our earnest desire is to become more fully, in His own
time, the one Church of Jesus Christ, united in faith,
communion, pastoral care and mission. Such unity is
the gift of God . . . We affirm our openness to this
growing unity . . .

Declaration of Churches Together
in England made at Swanwick, 1987

Prayers for the unity of the Church

We give thanks, our Father, for the unity
which is already ours as Christians.
We thank you that there is
one Body and one Spirit,
one hope which belongs to our calling,
one Lord, one faith, one baptism,
one God and Father of us all.
And we resolve by your grace that
Walking with all lowliness and meekness,
And forbearing one another in love,
We may maintain the unity of the Spirit
In the bond of peace,
Through Jesus Christ our Lord.

Frank Colquhoun, based on Ephesians 4.1-6

Lord of the Church
make the Church one,
and heal our divisions;
make the Church holy
in all her members and in all her branches;
make the Church catholic,
for all people and in all truth;
make the Church apostolic,
with the faith and mission of the first apostles.
We ask it in the name of Jesus Christ our Lord.

George Appleton

O Christ, may all that is a part of today's encounter be
born of the
Spirit of truth and be fruitful through love.
Behold before us: the past and the future.
Behold before us: the desires of so many hearts.
You, who are Lord of history and the Lord of human
hearts, be with us.
Christ Jesus, eternal Son of God, be with us.
Amen.

Prayer of Pope John Paul II
prayed in Canterbury Cathedral, 29 June 1982

What matters in the Church is not religion but
the form of Christ, and its taking form amidst a band
of people.

Dietrich Bonhoeffer

Holy Father,
protect them in your name that you have given
to me,
so that they may be one, as we are one.

John 17.11

The Outer Journey

7
Seeking the Kingdom

Power in complete subordination to love – that is
something like a definition of the Kingdom of God.

William Temple

Seek first the kingdom of God and everything else shall
be given to you.

Matthew 6.33

Learning to love

As God loves us, so we are called to love others. We are given strength for the great journey of Christian faith through our prayers and through the Scriptures; through Holy Communion and through our fellowship with other Christians. But we are called not to travel this journey for our own sake only but to share in God's mission to his world: to play our part in praying for and seeking and building the kingdom of God here on earth.

Throughout the gospels Jesus teaches about the kingdom of God. In Mark's gospel he bursts onto the scene proclaiming that God's kingdom is close at hand. His parables describe the kingdom as being like the yeast which leavens the dough, like a tiny mustard seed growing into a huge tree, like a merchant selling everything to obtain a fine pearl, like treasure hidden in a field, like a net cast into the sea.

It is a kingdom where the first will be last, and the last first. A kingdom which belongs to the poor in spirit and to those who are persecuted for righteousness' sake. Even at his death the thief hanging next to him on the cross has heard enough on the subject to cry out 'Remember me, Jesus, in that kingdom of yours!'

But how should we understand Jesus' teaching about the kingdom of God, and what does it mean for our lives as Christians today?

A kingdom without a king

The kingdom that Jesus establishes is a kingdom of beloved family members, not simply loyal subjects. We have already noted the radical import of Jesus calling God Father. Thus we see that this is a kingdom without a king: an inheritance where everyone is a first-born heir, for all who are baptized into the death and resurrection of Jesus become his blood brothers and sisters.

Of course Jesus himself is often referred to as king, but even here we need to see that Jesus' kingship contrasts starkly with the way authority is wielded in the world. There is that astounding passage in John's gospel where we read that Jesus, on the night he was betrayed, 'knowing that the Father had put everything into his hands, and that he had come from God and was returning to God, got up from the table' not, as we might imagine, to place a throne in the midst of his disciples so as to receive their homage; instead he 'removed his outer garments and, taking a towel . . . began to wash his disciples' feet.' (John 13.3-5)

A realm without boundaries

It follows that the kingdom of God is not a geographic entity: it cannot be found on a map. Neither does it exist only in heaven or only on earth, only in the future or only in the past: it cannot be identified solely with the Church, but neither can the Church be understood except as a herald of the kingdom. Its boundaries are human hearts; it is measured by relationship to Jesus. By this we mean not just how we enter that relationship, but how we live it out. This is the main emphasis of this second part of the book: the outer journey of the Christian life is about living as a child of the kingdom of God.

Tomorrow's life today

This should be the catchphrase of all those seeking to live the Christian life. All that has been done for us in Jesus through his life, death and resurrection; and all that awaits us in the life that is to come, is given not just for our own fulfilment – though it is very fulfilling – but for the salvation of the world. God wants his kingdom to be known in every human heart, and in the heart of every human situation. This is God's great mission of love to which we are invited to participate as disciples of Jesus Christ. The Anglican Consultative Council has helpfully itemized it in this way:

- To proclaim the good news of the kingdom.
- To teach, baptize and nurture new believers.
- To respond to human need by loving service.
- To seek to transform the unjust structures of society.
- To strive to safeguard the integrity of creation and sustain and renew the life of the earth.

This is known as the five marks of mission. It could equally be called the five signs of the kingdom. When we pray 'Your kingdom come, your will be done,' this is what we mean. We try to see the world as God sees it; we try to build the world as God longs it to be; we try to live our lives, and shape the life of the world, around the values and standards of God.

This will not be easy. As we see elsewhere in this book it will lead to conflict – because the world does not live by the standards of the gospel – and to mockery, for many people will make fun of us because we follow Christ. But it is vital that the Church of Jesus Christ lives out and proclaims the whole gospel of salvation, otherwise our faith is in danger of becoming a private option for individuals who like that sort of thing, and not the saving justice for the whole world which is God's mission in Jesus. Therefore wherever and whenever we see injustice, wherever and whenever we see the planet abused, human rights denied, people persecuted because of gender or colour or race or sexuality or creed, from how we fill in our tax return to the way we exercise our vote, to our righteous intolerance of the greed and pomp of the world, we need to stand up and live by the values of the kingdom of God, the life which is assured because of what God has done in Jesus, the life which we are called to embody to the world. The kingdom of God must be the touchstone by which all our activities as Christians are measured.

Of course Christianity and politics mix. The Christian faith is concerned with God's kingdom. As the writer to the Hebrews made it clear we are looking for a better city, 'whose architect and builder is God.' (Hebrews 11.10) It was because the prophets of the Old Testament had glimpsed God's glory and God's purpose that they thundered against social injustice and warned of impending doom. So the Church today must recover its prophetic witness to challenge the values of the world with the values of the kingdom of God. The kingdom of God is not just an interior experience. It is an interior experience of fellowship with God, but it is not only that. To live as a citizen of the kingdom is to be committed to the building of the kingdom here and now.

Turning the world the right way up

The earliest Christians were accused of turning the world upside
down as they sought to live as citizens of God's kingdom. But of
course they weren't: they were turning it the right way up, it's just
that we've got so used to the world the way it is, that when
people do seek to live as God intended, it appears absurd. But the
first Christians were ambassadors from God with a message of
righteousness, joy and peace (Paul's words to describe the kingdom
(Romans 14.17)) and they were also pioneers, mapping and building
a new humanity, a new civilization.

We need to be ambassadors and pioneers today: the world tells
us to look out for number one, to ration our affection, love only
those who will love in return, patrol the border and post the sentry.
The kingdom of God tells us to turn the other cheek, go the second
mile, lend without hope of return, give up the last coin, welcome
the stranger, forgive the sinner and love the enemy.

The world says what you see is what you get. The kingdom of God
says there's so much more – an abundant life, an extravagant love,
a full measure, pressed down and overflowing.

The world tries to turn children into adults, and in so doing we
imagine the world is ours and we can do with it what we want,
and live however we please. The kingdom of God tries to turn adults
into children, trusting God, abandoned to the joys of life lived in
the community of love, which is the fellowship of the Trinity.

So Jesus says if you want to enter the kingdom you must become
a little child. You must make yourself small, you must lose your life
in order to find it, you must re-learn delight in life, you must hunger
and thirst for righteousness, you must live passionately and intensely
in God's eternal now, and God's eternal yes to you: the sacrament of
this present moment, the kingdom of God.

Readings and prayers

He put before them another parable: 'The kingdom of
heaven is like a mustard seed that someone took and
sowed in his field; it is the smallest of all the seeds,
but when it has grown it is the greatest of shrubs and
becomes a tree, so that the birds of the air can come
and make nests in its branches.'

Matthew 13.31-32

A prayer for courage

Lord Jesus teach me to be generous;
teach me to serve you as you deserve,
to give and not to count the cost,
to fight and not to heed the wounds,
to toil and not to seek for rest,
to labour and not to ask for any reward,
except that of knowing that I do your will.

Ignatius of Loyola

He told them another parable: 'The kingdom of heaven
is like yeast that a woman took and mixed in with three
measures of flour until all of it was leavened.'

Matthew 13.33

For all who give you a face,
Lord Jesus,
by spreading your love in the world,
we praise you.

For all who give you hands,
Lord Jesus,
by doing their best towards their brothers and sisters,
we praise you.

For all who give you a mouth,
Lord Jesus,
by defending the weak and the oppressed,
we praise you.

For all who give you eyes,
Lord Jesus,
by seeing every bit of love,
we praise you.

For all who give you a heart,
Lord Jesus,
by preferring the poor to the rich,
the weak to the strong,
we praise you.

For all who give to your poverty,
Lord Jesus,
the look of hope for the Kingdom,
we praise you.

For all who reveal you
simply by what they are,
Lord Jesus,
because they reflect your beauty in their lives,
we praise you.

Lucien Deiss, *Come Lord Jesus*

Actually we are touching Christ's body in the poor.
In the poor it is the hungry Christ that we are feeding,
it is the naked Christ that we are clothing, it is the
homeless Christ that we are giving shelter.

Mother Teresa of Calcutta

The kingdom of heaven is like a merchant in search
of fine pearls; on finding one pearl of great value,
he went and sold all that he had and bought it.

Matthew 13.45-46

Though we achieve social justice, liberty, peace itself,
though we give our bodies to be burned for these
admirable causes, if we lack this – the transformation
of the natural order by the Eternal Charity – we are
nothing. For the kingdom is the Holy not the moral;
the Beautiful not the correct; the perfect not the
adequate; Charity not law.

Evelyn Underhill

Then the righteous will answer, 'Lord, when was it that
we saw you hungry and gave you food, or thirsty and
gave you something to drink? And when was it that
we saw you a stranger and welcomed you, or naked
and gave you clothing? And when was it that we saw
you sick or in prison and visited you?' And the king
will answer them, 'Truly I tell you, just as you did it to
one of the least of these who are members of my
family, you did it to me'.

Matthew 25.37-41

We wait for new heavens and a new earth, where
righteousness is at home.

2 Peter 3.13

8
Faith in Daily Life

He who labours as he prays lifts his heart to God with
his hands.

St Bernard of Clairvaux

Jesus said: 'I must stay at your house today.'

Luke 19.5

What does the Church do on Monday morning? We don't ask this question enough. The danger is that we worry so much about Sunday that we forget that the sustenance and energy we receive in worship is given to enable us to be the Church on Monday. The Church is us, the people of God, and what we do on Monday is what the Church does. And every Monday morning the Church is dispersed – to our homes, our places of work and our communities. It is here – in schools and colleges, factories and hospitals, prisons and supermarkets, sitting rooms and squash courts – that we are called to live the Christian life; and it is here that we are called to witness to the Christian faith. The best witness of all is a life lived to the full as God intends. This begins in the home, but overflows into our work and our leisure.

At home

The Jewish traditions which shaped Jesus' life, and which lie behind so much of the Christian faith, saw the home as the centre for spiritual life. It was in the home that children were taught the faith, and it was in the home that each Sabbath and the great festivals of the faith were celebrated. Hence, to this day, the great feast of the Passover is a family festival celebrated in the home.

The Early Church carried on these traditions. In the Acts of the Apostles we read about the first Christians meeting in each other's homes for worship and fellowship (Acts 2.46). In fact some of the earliest Christian communities were named after the people in whose homes the churches met. But now we use the word 'church' to describe a building, and so much of the observation of our faith has passed from the home to the church building. There is nothing intrinsically wrong with this. It is good for the Christian community to gather together. But we need a balance. Children growing up in Christian families need to experience faith as part of everyday life. All Christians need to be making connections between Sunday morning (or evening) 'church' and Monday morning life. If we look back into church history, or observe Christian communities in other parts of the world, we see faith being observed in the home in various ways which together shape the whole of life.

Emphasis on prayer together

We must strive to find ways of praying together with other Christians in our home and family. Once initial embarrassment has been overcome this is not nearly as intimidating as it sounds. It can begin with saying grace before a meal. In fact just having a meal together is a good place to start! So many people nowadays live together under the same roof but rarely eat together.

Rituals to celebrate the rhythm of each week and the Church year

This is particularly good with children. Lighting a candle each Sunday to accompany a meal or a time of prayer reminds us of the light of Easter. Friday could be recovered as a day of fasting for Christians. Fasting is a simple and practical way of praying. The word means 'doing without food' ('breakfast' each day is when we 'break the fast' of the previous night). We might miss a meal; do without something we particularly like for a short period; or eat more simply and dedicate the time and money saved to God. Fasting reminds us of the primacy of God – we experience everything, even food, as secondary to him. It reminds us of the needs of the world – so many of our brothers and sisters are without food: money that we save can go to them.

In the Christian year Advent (before Christmas) and Lent (before Easter) are particular seasons where we think about fasting and penitence. And giving something up, especially, marks Lent. Though taking something on as well would be a good idea.

Feasting is just as important as fasting: the Christian life is at heart a celebration. At Christmas prayer can accompany opening Advent calendars, putting up the tree, assembling the crib, sitting down to a special meal. At Easter a cross can be made, an Easter garden constructed, Easter eggs made and decorated. All these can become celebrations that pull faith into everyday life.

Signs of the Christian faith

The earliest Christian symbol was a fish. It was used as a secret sign to mark a Christian home or to show where the church was going to meet. The letters of the Greek word for 'fish' (ichthus) stand for 'Jesus Christ, Son of God, Saviour'. Today some Christians have this symbol on their cars, but it would be good to make more of our faith in the home. This is more evident in some traditions than others, but all Christians could at least have some sign in, or outside, their home to mark it as Christian. Furthermore, each Christian home could have its own 'holy place'. This could be very simple – a cross on the wall, an open Bible on a shelf, or, more elaborately, an actual place of prayer in the corner of a room. As long as it is in keeping with one's own tradition and culture it will be a focus and a reminder for living the faith each day. It will also tell visitors who is the most important person in the family!

These are all things we need to rediscover and translate into our own situations. They pull faith into daily life and stop faith being just that cerebral thing we do on Sunday.

But of course some of us are single and may feel alienated by these suggestions. Moreover, being single can mean all sorts of different things. For some it is a conscious decision; for others it is a consequence of what has often been a painful loss. And we are all single sometimes. Just as we should not blithely assume that family equals Mum and Dad and 2.2 children that we should not overlook the fact that many Christians have partners who do not share their faith. Therefore whether we are married or single, sharing faith with others in our household or not, we should all endeavour to make our home a place of witness and prayer in the way that is appropriate to our situation.

And if we are in a situation where our partner does not share our faith it is wise to remember that marriage is just as much a vocation as faith. Church should not take second place to family: God's love and God's call is total, and if God has called us to marriage and parenthood this is never superseded by other callings, but always enhanced. Of course we long for faith to be shared by those we love, but often the best witness is a quiet fortitude in Christian prayer and service, and a proper balance between the sometimes conflicting commitments of church and home.

At work

Faith is not a leisure pursuit. Being Christian shapes and informs the whole of life. And the whole of life includes the work we do. And while we must continue to resist that rather insidious tendency to define one another by our jobs – our first question to a new acquaintance is often 'what do you do?' – our work does represent a major part of our life, both in the time we spend working and the way it shapes the style and conditions of our life, for good or ill. But as Christians we would first want to affirm that work is so much more than paid employment. There is a dignity to work that extends beyond status and salary. Often the work that contributes the most good to society is the most poorly rewarded. And often it is hidden. Society may not seem to value the devoted care of a good neighbour watching out for an elderly person in their street; a young mum waking early to tend to her children's needs; a pensioner tilling the soil of his allotment, but God does! Our work is what we do; it is those activities that mark and occupy our day. Our work is an offering to God, a sign of our co-creativity with him, and whatever we do, we should seek to do it to the best of our ability and with as much joy as we can muster.

In this sense we can pray through our work, making what we do, however menial, a fount of praise. Brother Lawrence, who lived in the eighteenth century, spent much of his time in the monastery working in the kitchen, but, by trying to make each action of his work a communion with God, he developed a form of prayer, and a way of working, which he called the 'practice of the presence of God'. This shaped his life and comes to us as an encouragement to pray through all the rhythms of our daily life and to offer our work to God.

However, there is some work where it is very hard to see God. Many people are exploited in the work they do. Some are involved in industries whose success depends upon the exploitation of people in other parts of the world. The wealth that many enjoy is often dependent upon the poverty of others. Despite the rhetoric of goodwill, Third World countries are still crippled by debt. Changing patterns of work mean that those who have employment are often working under increasing pressure with scant reward and little long-term security. Some enjoy huge and disproportionate rewards for the work they do, and others are unemployed, resigned to a life of diminishing opportunities, and denied the material benefits and luxuries that economic prosperity provides. And the distorted values of our society mean that many are rightly indignant that their work and contribution is valued so slightly. These are issues Christians need to be more concerned about. Therefore, all that has been said about finding God in the actions of work should not deter us from also seeking justice in our work; from opposing those distortions which pervert our society and by working for a world where dignity, respect and opportunity are returned to all.

At play

The concept of leisure for everyone is fairly new. Until recently, unless you were very well-off then life meant sleep and work. There was little room for much else. But society has changed radically and in the West our prosperity allows most of us to divide our time into leisure as well as work. In fact our society has created a whole leisure industry – even the busiest people at work are also busy with leisure.

Just as faith permeates our home and our work, so it can inform our play. Here is a great opportunity to be creative and to discover precious, and often neglected, aspects of ourselves. And surely one of the great signs of being made in the image of God is this creativity which each of us possesses and which is expressed in marvellously different ways according to our gifts and personality.

God made life to be enjoyed. He made us with different gifts. Often it is at our leisure that we can really exploit these to God's glory – and this can be done by arranging flowers, running a marathon, playing chess, growing a prize marrow, or building a scale model of Westminster Abbey out of matchsticks! It does not really matter what thing you do, as long as it is your thing – the way of being you that God has gifted.

One important Christian insight to bring to our leisure is that there is more to life than striving for excellence all the time and competing with others. G.K. Chesterton, the great Christian writer and thinker, said, 'If a thing is worth doing, it is worth doing badly!' In other words, yes, do it as best you can, but if it is worth doing then it is worth doing for its own sake, and is not dependent on how good you are.

There are dangerous and indulgent uses of leisure, and these can be harmful and self-destructive. But leisure which enables us to enjoy the fullness of life brings us very close to the God who crowned his creation not with labour but with Sabbath: the opportunity to enter into joy, to participate in all that has been made, because it is very good. In the words of St Paul: 'So, whether you eat or drink, or whatever you do, do everything for the glory of God' (1 Corinthians 10.31).

Readings and prayers

> Whatever your work is, put your heart into it, as done
> for the Lord and not for human beings, knowing that the
> Lord will repay you by making you his heirs. It is Christ
> the Lord that you are serving.
>
> Colossians 3.23-24 (*New Jerusalem Bible*)

> For Christians are distinguished from other people
> neither by country nor by language nor by customs. For
> nowhere do they dwell in cities of their own; they do not
> use any strange form of speech or practise a singular
> mode of life. This lore of theirs has not been discovered
> by any design and thought of prying men, nor do they
> champion a mere human doctrine, as some people do.
> But while they dwell in both Greek and barbarian cities,

each as his lot is cast, and follow the customs of the land
in dress and food and other matters of living, they show
forth the remarkable and admittedly strange order of
their citizenship. They live in fatherlands of their own,
but as aliens. They share all things as citizens, and
suffer all things as strangers. Every foreign land is their
fatherland, and every fatherland foreign land. They marry,
like all others; they breed children, but do not cast out
their offspring. Free board they provide, but no carnal
bed. They are 'in the flesh' but they do not live 'after
the flesh'. They pass their days on earth, but they have
citizenship in heaven. They obey the appointed laws,
yet in their own lives they excel the laws. They love all
people, and are persecuted by all. They are unknown, yet
they are condemned; they are put to death, yet they are
made alive. 'They are poor, yet they make many rich'. They
suffer the lack of all things, yet they abound in all things.
They are dishonoured, yet are glorified in their dishonour.
They are evil spoken of, yet they are vindicated. 'They are
reviled, and they bless'; insulted, they repay with honour.
When doing good they are punished as evildoers;
suffering punishment, they rejoice as if quickened into
life . . . Yet those who hate them cannot state the cause
of their hostility. Broadly speaking what the soul is in
the body, that Christians are in the world.

The Epistle to Diognetus

The glory of God is a human being fully alive.

St Irenaeus

A prayer of blessing on the home

Visit this house, O Lord we pray,
drive far from it all the snares of the enemy;
may your holy angels dwell with us
and guard us in peace
and may your blessing always be upon us;
through Jesus Christ our Lord. Amen.

The Prayer Book as Proposed in 1928

Grace before and after meals

In a world where so many are hungry we thank you
for food,
In a world where so many are lonely we thank you
for friends.
Amen.

The Lord gives food to those who fear him:
He is ever mindful of his promises.

Psalm 111.5

The eyes of all wait upon you Lord:
You give them their food in due season.

Psalm 104.27

Jesus said, 'Therefore I tell you, do not worry about your
life, what you will eat or what you will drink, or about
your body, what you will wear. Is not life more than
food, and the body more than clothing? Look at the
birds of the air; they neither sow nor reap nor gather
into barns, and yet your heavenly Father feeds them. Are
you not of more value than they? And can any of you by
worrying add a single hour to your span of life? And
why do you worry about clothing? Consider the lilies of
the field, how they grow; they neither toil nor spin, yet

I tell you, even Solomon in all his glory was not clothed as one of these. But if God so clothes the grass of the field, which is alive today and tomorrow is thrown into the oven, will he not much more clothe you – you of little faith? Therefore do not worry, saying, ' What will we eat?' or 'What will we drink?' or 'What will we wear?' For it is the Gentiles who strive for all these things; and indeed your heavenly Father knows that you need all these things. But strive first for the kingdom of God and his righteousness, and all these things will be given to you as well. So do not worry about tomorrow, for tomorrow will bring worries of its own. Today's trouble is enough for today.'

Matthew 6.25-34

Christ has no body
now on earth but yours,
no hands but yours,
no feet but yours.

Yours are the eyes
through which must look out
Christ's compassion on the world.

Yours are the feet with which
He is to go about doing good.

Yours are the hands with which
He is to bless people now.

St Teresa of Avila

Loving God, source of order and form in life: inspire us
in our work that we may constantly seek your guidance,
acknowledge your presence, and daily strive to serve you
faithfully; for Jesus' sake. Amen.

adapted from Dick Williams

9
Serving God

Will you seek and serve Christ in all people,
loving your neighbour as yourself?

Common Worship: Holy Baptism

No one can serve two masters: for a slave will
either hate this one and love the other, or be devoted
to that one and despise the other. You cannot serve
God and wealth.

Matthew 5.24

Offering our lives to God

Christian faith is not about filling a hole in our lives but involves the whole of our lives. Unless Jesus Christ is Lord of all, then he is not Lord at all. To worship God on Sunday means offering him our lives on Monday and each day that follows in gratitude and thanksgiving for all he has done for us. Leisure is important. But the Christian faith is not a hobby or leisure interest.

The first generation of Christians were used to a form of worship in Judaism which involved the offering of sacrifices. To come to worship meant that you brought some grain or wine or an animal to a temple. This was then offered up to God, often through being burnt or poured out on the altar.

In the Early Church there was no system of sacrificing animals or making other kinds of offerings in the Temple or in worship. Christians believe that Jesus Christ gave up his life as the perfect sacrifice, a once and for all event that could never be repeated to reconcile God and his creation. In response to God's love in Christ, Christians are called to offer not their possessions but their whole lives in service:

> I appeal to you therefore, brothers and sisters, by the mercies of God, to present your bodies as a living sacrifice, holy and acceptable to God, which is your spiritual worship.
>
> Romans 12.1

We pray together at the end of every service of Holy Communion:

> Almighty God,
> we thank you for feeding us
> with the body and blood of your Son Jesus Christ.
> Through him we offer you our souls and bodies
> to be a living sacrifice.

Send us out
in the power of your Spirit
to live and work
to your praise and glory.
Amen.

Common Worship: Holy Communion
(Prayer after Communion)

Particular gifts

Every Christian is called to serve God and others. But we are all called
to serve in different ways. The Bible speaks of every Christian being
given different gifts. Those with different gifts are of equal value in
the life of the Church but will express their Christian service in very
different ways. Sometimes these gifts will be natural aptitudes or
talents. Sometimes they will be, in part, the product of training
or life experience or even suffering. Sometimes they will be graces
given by God the Holy Spirit as part of our Christian experience: a
gift to share in the ministry of healing, or to pass on Christian faith,
or to teach others. Examples of different kinds of gifts are given in
different places in the New Testament. Jesus' teaching in the parable
of the 'talents' is that God asks us to make the best use of the time,
energy, health and particular gifts we have been given in our lives,
like good stewards. One day we will be asked to give account of the
way in which we have used these treasures in our Christian service.

One of the great mysteries of the Christian life is a very common
sense Christians have of being called to a particular task, lifestyle or
job by God for all or part of our lives. Christians call this a vocation
(from the Latin word meaning 'to call'). Every Christian should try to
be open to discovering what God may be calling them to do at each
different stage of their lives and particularly where big decisions are
being made.

Serving God in daily life

Serving God does not mean, necessarily, doing new things or extra
things and must not mean only what I do 'at church'. First and
foremost it means a different way of seeing the ordinary things

I am doing now. My daily work becomes not simply something I do for myself but something which can be offered to God. Voluntary work in the community or for charity is an expression of Christian service, offered again to God and to others. Looking after an elderly relative; patiently caring for young children; listening to my neighbour; befriending the stranger in the community; serving on the local council: all of these things are aspects of Christian service.

As we grow in our Christian lives, as we worship and as we pray, so our living becomes less centred on ourselves and meeting our own needs and more concerned with meeting the needs of others. The more we are consciously serving God in daily living and giving out to others, the more we will need to be sustained by worship, prayer and fellowship with other Christians.

Service in the life of the Church

For most Christians, at least part of our Christian service will be offered in and through the life of our local church. In most churches, there are plenty of opportunities to get involved in simple, practical acts of service which build community and help in some way or other. You may find that help is needed in your own church in simple tasks such as cleaning, helping with the maintenance of buildings or grounds, making coffee after services or providing a welcome at Sunday services. Most people find that making a contribution in some way helps them to feel they belong and is a help in getting to know others.

As you grow in your Christian life, and as your gifts are recognized by others, you may be asked to help in other ways depending upon the needs in your congregation at a particular time. Help may be needed with the Parent and Toddler Group; with groups of children on Sundays or in a crèche. You may be asked to become a sponsor for an adult enquiring about Christian faith or to visit a housebound person. You may have the opportunity to become part of a team visiting homes in the parish, working with those bringing children for baptism or with the bereaved. You may have musical gifts which can be offered in worship or secretarial or financial skills. Others may

There are different ways of serving God within the structures of the church. Every Anglican parish has two churchwardens, who are officers of the Bishop, and a Parochial Church Council (PCC) who embody the shared responsibility of clergy and laity working together within a parish. The Church of England also has a structure of elected government at local and national level – deanery, diocesan and general synods. As well as a variety of ministries exercised at parish level, some lay ministers are licensed by the bishop including readers and, in some dioceses, pastoral assistants and evangelists.

recognize your gifts and ask you to consider serving on the church council.

In some of these areas, the church may offer some training at parish or diocesan level. If you are invited to consider working with children, bear in mind that the church, like all voluntary organizations, has to follow national guidelines on issues such as child protection. If you are asked to consider doing anything in the life of the church, take some time to think about it and pray about whether it seems right or not. Beware of taking on too much too soon. As with any new commitment, make sure you leave yourself sufficient time and energy for family and work commitments and community involvement. Don't be afraid to say 'no' – and offer whatever you can with the attitude of a servant, the attitude of Christ. That means you should avoid wanting to show off your gifts and abilities or pushing yourself to the front. Allow your ministry within the life of the church to grow naturally and with time: the most valuable acts of service are often the ones which are hidden from public view.

Ordained ministry

From the very beginning of the Church, individuals have been set aside for the task of serving and enabling the whole Christian community in its worship and mission. Different churches have used different names for those who are ordained: ministers, priests, elders and so on and have evolved different ways of recognizing their ministries.

In the Church of England, ministers are ordained by a bishop with the laying on of hands and through prayer to this particular kind of Christian service. This ordination can only take place after a process of selection for ministry at local and national level and a period of preparation and training which lasts several years.

Some ordained ministers in the Church of England are fulltime and paid for their work. Others are known as self-supporting ministers (SSMs) or non-stipendiary ministers (NSMs): they are not paid for their ministry directly but offer it voluntarily and support themselves by other means. In some dioceses of the Church of England there are also ordained local ministers (OLMs) who are ordained to serve in one particular parish or place, usually as part of a local ministry team.

All clergy in the Church of England are ordained *deacon*. The word 'deacon' means servant. The ministry of a deacon is based upon service lovingly offered both within the church and the wider community. Most clergy are also ordained *priest* or *presbyter* some time later. The ministry of a priest is concerned with sustaining the whole community of faith through the ministry of the word (study, preaching and teaching the faith to others) and the ministry of the sacraments (particularly of baptism and Holy Communion).

All of the clergy in a particular diocese are responsible to and work with the *bishop*, who is charged with safeguarding the unity and sound teaching of the Christian community and leading and enabling its mission.

The gift of giving

As part of our stewardship, all Christians are called to offer not only our time and talents to God but also our money and possessions. This will involve, for all of us, carefully and responsibly reflecting on how we will give to our local church to support its life, work and mission and how we will give to other good causes. We need to be prepared to give responsibly rather than casually: thinking in advance about how we should give and how the church and other organizations can derive the most benefit from what is given. Your church treasurer will gladly supply you with more details.

And finally . . .

Jesus said that he came not to be served but to serve and to give his life for others. On the night before he was crucified, the Son of God laid aside his robes, took a towel and a basin of water and washed the dirty, tired feet of his disciples and wiped them with the towel. Afterwards he said to them

> Do you know what I have done to you? You call me
> Teacher and Lord – and you are right, for that is what
> I am. So if I, your Lord and Teacher, have washed your
> feet, you also ought to wash one another's feet. For
> I have set you an example that you also should do as
> I have done to you.
>
> John 13.12-15

Readings and prayers

> I am no longer my own, but yours.
> Put me to what you will,
> rank me with whom you will.
> Put me to doing, put me to suffering.
> Let me be employed for you, or laid aside for you.
> Let me be full, let me be empty;
> let me have all things, let me have nothing.
> I freely and gladly yield all things
> to your pleasure and disposal.
> And now, O glorious and blessed God,
> Father, Son and Holy Spirit,
> you are mine and I am yours. So be it.
> And the Covenant which I have made on earth,
> let it be ratified in heaven.
> Amen.
>
> *The Methodist Service Book*

I will offer up my life in spirit and truth
pouring out the oil of love as my worship to you.
In surrender I must give my every part,
Lord receive the sacrifice of a broken heart.

Jesus what can I give, what can I bring
to so faithful a friend to so loving a king?
Saviour what can be said, what can be sung
As a praise of your name for the things you have done.
Oh my words could not tell not even in part
of the debt of love that is owed by this thankful heart.

You deserve my every breath for you've paid the great
cost giving up your life to death, even death on a cross.
You took all my shame away, there defeated my sin,
opened up the gates of heaven and have beckoned me in.

Matt Redman

Too often I have looked at being relevant, popular, and
powerful as ingredients of an effective ministry. The truth,
however, is that these are not vocations but temptations.
Jesus asks, 'Do you love me?' Jesus sends us out to be
shepherds, and Jesus promises a life in which we
increasingly have to stretch out our hands and be led to
places where we would rather not go. He asks us to move
from a concern for relevance to a life of prayer, from
worries about popularity to communal and mutual
ministry, and from leadership built on power to a
leadership in which we critically discern where God
is leading us.

Henri Nouwen

New every morning is the love
Our wakening and uprising prove,
Through sleep and darkness safely brought
Restored to life and power and thought.

New mercies, each returning day
Hover around us while we pray;
New perils past, new sins forgiven,
New thoughts of God, new hopes of heaven.

If on our daily course our mind
Be set to hallow all we find,
New treasures still of countless price,
God will provide for sacrifice.

The trivial round, the common task,
Will furnish all we ought to ask,
Room to deny ourselves, a road
To bring us daily nearer God.

Only, O Lord in thy dear love
Fit us for perfect rest above;
And help us this and every day,
To live more nearly as we pray.

> John Keble, from his poem 'Hues of the Rich
> Unfolding Morn' in *The Christian Year*

Prayer for the ministry of all Christian people

Almighty and everlasting God,
by whose spirit the whole body of the Church
   is governed and sanctified:
hear our prayer which we offer for all your
   faithful people,
that in their vocation and ministry
they may serve you in holiness and truth
to the glory of your name;
through our Lord and Saviour Jesus Christ,
who is alive and reigns with you,
in the unity of the Holy Spirit,
one God, now and for ever.

The Christian Year: Collects and Post Communion
Prayers for Sundays and Festivals

10
Christian Witness

Put your heart into being a bright light.

Mother Teresa of Calcutta

As the Father has sent me, so I send you.

John 20.21

Every Christian is called to be a witness to Jesus. Whether we like it or not once people discover that we go to church they will be making judgements about the Christian faith based upon the evidence of our life. This does not mean that we make ourselves out to be better than other people. This only plays into the hands of that popular misconception of Christianity, which equates being a Christian with being good. Of course, we strive to live a good life, but what marks us out as Christian is not our virtue – clearly there are many people who do not go to church whose lives are just as virtuous as ours – but God's grace. We are Christians not because of what our goodness has achieved, but because of the mercy God has lavished upon us. We know just how bad we have been. We know just how great is our need of forgiveness. We know that when we were far off, God has come and sought us out. Our faith is not something we have earned by our merit, but something we have received by grace.

Therefore, we are graceful to others. We, of all people, should be more loving, more forgiving, more tolerant, more gentle, more steadfast in what we believe and how we put it into practice, and more prepared to go the second mile with those who stumble and fall, and with those who are far from God. These are the marks of a Christian life which should be evident to others – a readiness to admit failing and need, and an eagerness to deal with others with the same graceful humility with which God has dealt with us. Over time the witness of faithful Christian lifestyle can make a huge difference, even if we often do not see the results ourselves. This can be particularly true in family life, when overt witness is not always the best way forward.

But in this matter none of us can say, 'Oh I don't have that particular calling.' The real question we are faced with is not 'am I a witness to Jesus?' – as we can see, we have no choice on that one – but 'what sort of witness is Jesus calling me to be?' And here we should not confuse the word 'witness' with 'evangelist'. This is, indeed, a particular calling. But a life lived with faith, hope and love, the supreme gifts of God's spirit (1 Corinthians 13.13), will not only be a joyful life, a life of purpose, a life without regret, it will be a powerful witness to the gospel. It will be the best evangelism of all.

However, we live in a world that is both challenged and offended by the gospel. These are two areas that require particular thought and attention as we travel the Christian way.

Naming Jesus

In the course of daily life we will encounter people who are inspired by the gospel, and in particular by the person of Jesus. This will happen in all sorts of ways – a programme on television, a birth in the family, a crisis in the world, an illness, the onset of a new year, the death of a loved one. On these occasions we are the ones who are called to help people make the connection between the stirrings of their heart and the good news of Jesus Christ.

Often people are yearning to articulate a heartfelt plea or thanks to God, but embarrassment gets in the way. Or else they are prevented by their own half-formed conceptions of God. Some do not feel worthy; thinking God is only interested in so-called 'good' people. Others can't believe in a God who is interested and involved, let alone one who can actually help. And saddest of all many people turn elsewhere for comfort and meaning. The human spirit longs for communion with God and will therefore seek some scraps of succour wherever they are to be found. Thus we see the growing interest in other ways of making sense of life, from the relatively harmless – horoscopes and the like – to the more disturbing distortions of some New Age practices. But if people are thirsty, and if the way to the living water is cut off, they will drink whatever is available. The challenge here is to the Church. Together we must strive to refresh our proclamation of the Christian faith so it becomes again good news, speaking directly and powerfully to the human heart.

For most of our society allegiance to the Christian faith is relegated to a private option – perfectly OK for those who like that sort of thing, but not necessarily of relevance to anyone else. But if the gospel is true then it must be true for every person. And if Jesus Christ is good news for one person, then he must be good news for every person. Either that, or it is not true, and not good news.

But we must also receive this challenge as individuals. People need help to see that it is God they are longing for, and it is only with God that they can find the satisfaction they seek. This does not mean endlessly banging on about God, but it does mean, as the Scriptures say, always being ready to give a reason for your hope (see 1 Peter 3.15). This is the help we can offer as witnesses to Jesus. Not just the lives we lead, but also the words we say so that at those God-given moments in life when people are open to receive the gift of faith we can help them see the treasures that God is offering.

Again and again in the New Testament we read of Paul praying that God will open a door of opportunity for the gospel (Colossians 4.3 and others). This should also be our prayer. We all have networks of family, friends, colleagues and neighbours. We should pray for these people. We should serve them as if they were Christ.

Here are some very practical ways of being a witness to people we know in daily life:

- Pray for the people with whom you have regular contact. Write out a list of people you could be praying for regularly.

- When you meet them consider what things you could be praying for in their life.

- Consider if there are practical ways that you can help them, i.e. baby-sitting or mowing the lawn.

- Invite them to an appropriate event at your church.

- Lend them a book or video or tape.

We should also be alert to opportunities to tell people about Christ. This telling need not be preaching, nor lecturing, but simply sharing the story of our faith.

All of us have two unique and wonderful stories to share with others – the story of what God has done in Jesus, and the story of what God has done in us. It is the particular ministry of witness to tell this latter story as a way of encouraging others on their journey to God. Therefore we need to ponder on our story. How has God been at work in our life? How did God find us? What is he doing and saying through our life that speaks of the hope he offers to all? In this way we will be ready to witness to Christ in his continuing mission of love to the world.

Helping people come to faith

We also need to be aware that all of the research done in recent years on how people become Christians, and the overwhelming experience of churches who have engaged seriously with evangelism, is that most people come to faith gradually over quite a long period of time. It is like a journey.

Usually there are key events along the way, but most new Christians point to two things as being fundamental to their journey. First, the witness of other Christian people – friends, family members, colleagues. Secondly, stepping-stone events provided by the local church that allowed them to discover more about the church and the life of faith and which then led to an opportunity to explore what faith was all about alongside other enquirers and committed Christians.

Some of this may resonate with your own experience of becoming a Christian. We therefore need to be encouraged in the part that we can play in God's work of evangelism (fortunately, he is the one who brings people to faith, not us!); and also encouraged to think about how our church provides those stepping-stone events and a place of exploration and discovery where faith and a community of belief can be encountered.

Facing persecution

But there are also times when the gospel confounds. Our society does not live by the standards of the Christian faith, and nor does any other society. Everywhere we look we see the distressing fruits of greed and pride. And while we naturally long for a peaceful, stress-free life, Jesus has made it clear that those who seek his peace will be persecuted for their troubles. In fact the very word 'witness' carries in the Greek language in which the New Testament was written the double meaning of testifier, the one who gives evidence of what they have seen and experienced, and martyr, the one who suffers and is killed for the witness they bear. This is a painful truth for us to carry. But it does save us from the twin dangers of complacency and triumphalism that so often bedevil missionary endeavour.

We need to be realistic about the world we live in, and the forces set against us. There will be times when we are mocked and ridiculed for our faith and times when we will wish we could hide it, or even cast it away. There may even be times, as there are for many thousands of Christians around the world, when we may face actual, physical persecution on account of the gospel. When these things happen – however dark or desperate we feel – we need to be steadfast in the faith we have received, remembering that we are not to be concerned by the worldly estimates of success or failure, only faithfulness to God's will, and thankfulness for his love. Just because we may not be successful in attracting large numbers of people to church – indeed, even if numbers continue to decline – this does not mean we stop evangelizing. Nor does it mean we do not have a vital witness to individuals and society. Nor does it call into question the truth or relevance of the gospel.

Shining brightly

Paul speaks of some being called to be evangelists (Ephesians 4.11). As we already pointed out, that will be the specific calling of some Christians whom God gifts in a particular way to make the gospel known and bring people to faith. But Paul goes on to explain that all are called to pattern their life on Christ:

> Be imitators of God, as beloved children, and live in love as Christ loved us and gave himself up for us.
>
> Ephesians 5.1–2

This is a description of the witness. The person whose life speaks of Christ. This is the evangelistic calling which comes to each of us because we belong to Christ. When we were baptized we put on Christ and, as a sign of our new calling, were presented with a candle with the instruction to 'Shine as a light in the world'.

Readings and prayers

They will hand you over to councils and flog you in their
synagogues; and you will be dragged before governors
and kings because of me, as a testimony to them and
the Gentiles. When they hand you over, do not worry
about how you are to speak or what you are to say; for
what you are to say will be given to you at that time;
for it is not you who speak, but the Spirit of your Father
speaking through you.

Matthew 10.17–20

The prayer of a witness to Jesus

Dear Lord, help me to spread thy fragrance everywhere
I go. Flood my soul with thy spirit and life. Penetrate and
possess my whole being so utterly that all my life may
only be a radiance of thine. Shine through me, and be
so in me that every soul I come in contact with may feel
thy presence in my soul.

Let them look up and see no longer me, but only thee,
O Lord! Stay with me, and then I shall begin to shine as
thou shinest; so to shine as to be a light to others.

The light O Lord will be all from thee; none of it will be
mine; it will be thou, shining on others through me. Let
me thus praise thee in the way thou dost love best, by
shining on those around me.

Let me preach thee without preaching, not by words
but by my example, by the catching force, the
sympathetic influence of what I do, the evident
fullness of the love my heart bears to thee. Amen.

adapted by Mother Teresa of Calcutta from
the prayer by Cardinal Newman

A prayer of self-offering

Lord Jesus,
   I give you my hands to do your work.
   I give you my feet to go your way.
   I give you my eyes to see as you do.
   I give you my tongue to speak as you do.
   I give you my mind that you may think in me.
   I give you my spirit that you may pray in me.
Above all
   I give you my heart that you may live in me,
   Your Father, and all humankind.
   I give you my whole self that you may grow in me,
   So that it is you, Lord Jesus,
   Who live and work and pray in me.

A prayer inviting God to use us in the ministry of evangelism

Loving God,
make my life a sign of your engaging love:
   may my heart be penitent,
   my actions generous,
   my words sensitive.
Fill me with longing to share with others the good
news I have received,
and anoint my life with your Spirit that Jesus be
formed in me:
   his tongue to speak in me
   his hands to work in me
   his heart to beat in me.
And so through all I do, and all I am,
   and with the people where you call me to witness,
   may Jesus be known
   and his kingdom established.

Stephen Cottrell

And to what shall we compare the church's evangelists? They need to be shepherds who know where their sheep are and who can find them, without driving them further from the fold. They need to be news announcers who get the message straight and who make it known clearly to the nations without resorting to sensationalism . . . They need to be lawyers who can argue their client's case with integrity, good humour and grit. They need to be midwives who can help nature and grace bring children of God to birth through the pain of repentance and the joy of faith. They need to be physicians of the soul who can link the lost and weary with the healing medicine of the kingdom. They need to be mothers who bring their little ones to be bathed in the waters of baptism, to be fed by word and creed at the breasts of mother church, to be drenched in the gifts of the Spirit, and to be equipped with the oil of prayer and fasting.

William Abraham

When the Advocate comes, whom I will send to you from the Father, the Spirit of truth who comes from the Father, he will testify on my behalf. You also are to testify.

John 15.26-27

11
In Times of Difficulty

My God, my God, why have you forsaken me?
Why are you so far from helping me, from the words
of my groaning?

Psalm 22.1

Man was made for Joy and Woe;
And when this we rightly know
Thro' the World we safely go.
Joy and Woe are woven fine,
A Clothing for the Soul divine;
Under every grief and pine
Runs a joy with silken twine.

William Blake, *Auguries of Innocence*

O God,
you know us to be set
   in the midst of so many and great dangers,
that by reason of the frailty of our nature
we cannot always stand upright:
grant to us such strength and protection
as may support us in all dangers
and carry us through all temptations;
through Jesus Christ our Lord.

*The Christian Year: Collects and Post Communion Prayers
for Sundays and Festivals (Fourth Sunday Before Lent)*

Rowing upstream is more demanding that drifting with the flow of the river. Climbing a mountain is harder than walking a wide, smooth pathway which leads gently downhill. Sitting on the sofa watching a game of football asks very little of us: step onto the field and begin playing the game and it's a different matter. Visit a famous, carefully kept garden and take in the order and beauty at little cost to yourself. To reproduce that garden in your own back yard demands patient labour over many years.

When we became Christians we began that lifetime's work which is Christian discipleship: living according to the way of Jesus. To follow that way with my whole heart is a demanding and costly way of living.

Jesus speaks in different places:

- of the narrow gate and the hard way which lead to life (Matthew 7.14);

- of the need for every disciple to deny themselves, take up their cross and follow him (Mark 8.34);

- of the need for everyone who becomes a Christian to count the cost before we begin the journey (Luke 14.28);

- of the need for each branch of the vine which bears fruit to be pruned as part of its growth (John 15.2).

For the early Christians, suffering was a common experience.

Following the pattern of Christ, within a few years of the resurrection, a Christian named Stephen was stoned to death in Jerusalem for witnessing to his faith and became the first of many martyrs, those who were killed for their Christian belief (the word 'martyr' means, simply, a witness). The story is told in Acts 6 and 7. The letters of the New Testament and the Book of Revelation are full of encouragement to the young Churches to be steadfast and endure suffering for the sake of the gospel. Those in Christian ministry in particular are called to costly discipleship:

> But we have this treasure in clay jars, so that it may be made clear that this extraordinary power belongs to God and does not come from us. We are afflicted in every way, but not crushed; perplexed, but not driven to despair; persecuted, but not forsaken; struck down, but not destroyed; always carrying in the body the death of Jesus, so that the life of Jesus may also be made visible in our bodies. For while we live, we are always being given up to death for Jesus' sake, so that the life of Jesus may be made visible in our mortal flesh.
>
> 2 Corinthians 4.7-11

As Christians we cannot escape or avoid the bad things which might happen to anyone in this life: illness and injury; poverty and accidents; hurt in relationships or hurting others; disability; bereavement and death. We live in an imperfect world where suffering is part of the fabric of every life: to suppose that the Christian life guarantees immunity from pain and difficulty is to make a very serious mistake which may lead one day to disappointment and bitterness. In addition, there will be some difficulties which arise particularly from living life as a Christian: the desert times of our spiritual experience when God seems far away; times when our faith is challenged by doubts and questions, not least those which arise from suffering; struggles against temptation or with guilt; the hidden cost of honesty and integrity; sometimes outright persecution because of our faith.

The words of the Bible and of Christians who have travelled this way before us are not given so that we can avoid suffering and difficulty but they are a source of tremendous comfort, strength and support within that suffering. What resources has the Christian faith to bring to these times of difficulty?

Truth

The first help is the perspective of honesty: truthfulness about our lives in relation to one another and to God. Sometimes Christians feel as though they must keep a stiff upper lip, or, even worse, a cheesy grin through all situations of grief, pain and difficulty. We begin to wear a mask of pretence in our relationships with others and our relationship with God. Behind that mask we groan with pain or cry with anger or hurt.

This dishonesty is a distortion of Christian faith. Jesus is the one who says, 'I am the truth'. Our lives will contain at least some bad times and bad events. We cannot begin to deal with them until we acknowledge them and name them.

Of all the books in the Bible, the Psalms are the most help to us here. Some of the psalms are great symphonies of joy and praise or quiet prayers of confidence. But many are laments which use words of biting honesty to express pain, grief, anguish and doubt to God on behalf of a community and of individuals. Praying in the words of the psalms teaches us that God is big enough to handle all of our doubts, questions, worries, jealousy, grief and rage and that all of these emotions need to be owned and given voice in our prayers and, sometimes, in our worship. The Book of Job in the Old Testament is an extended meditation on suffering which contains no easy answers but which commends honesty and integrity rather than cheap advice or pretence. When I come to God, it must be as a real person living a real life: not a sanitized individual living in some kind of fantasy world in which everything is absolutely fabulous. If something hurts, or provokes you to questions or anger, or God seems far away then admit it to yourself, to God himself and to other people.

Love

The second perspective to keep is that of love. Our suffering may be very deep and at times may be the largest element in our lives. God's love for us is deeper still and holds us in the midst of that suffering.

How do we know that God's love is of such a quality? Because of Jesus Christ and his death on the cross. The love of God is demonstrated there in a way which passes understanding. God's love is no arm's length expression of devotion which costs nothing and is soon forgotten. God's love revealed in Christ is about a commitment to us which is deeper than the universe demonstrated in his suffering and death on our behalf; a commitment stronger than any human tie or affection; a desire for our good and well being and salvation which is deeper than any human desire we can know; a solidarity with us, whatever we have done, which will last for all eternity. Paul writes:

> For I am convinced that neither death, nor life, nor angels, nor rulers, nor things present, nor things to come, nor powers, nor height, nor depth, nor anything else in all creation, will be able to separate us from the love of God in Christ Jesus our Lord.
>
> Romans 8.38

In times of great emotional and physical pain or distress especially, we may not be able to discover any sense of God's love for us in the way we feel or when we pray. In such times especially we need to remember that the Christian life is about faith: trusting in God's promises. In such times, ideally, we will need to find the love of God mediated through the love and care of those around us. In such times we will find the sacraments, and especially Holy Communion, particularly helpful: God's love becomes present to us in bread and wine giving strength for the next part of the journey.

Perseverance

Any worthwhile enterprise in life demands commitment over time. If you are learning to drive; building up your own business; working for exams; developing a relationship or improving your physical fitness you will hit times when, for one reason or another, the venture becomes very difficult and you are tempted to give up. Any good coach (in any of these areas) would give the same advice at these times: keep going. The New Testament writers give exactly the same counsel to Christians in every generation whenever they hit large or small difficulties in their journey. Don't be diverted. Persevere.

In one of Jesus' best-known parables, a sower goes out and sows seed which lands in four kinds of soil. Some lands on the path and is eaten by the birds immediately. It never begins to grow. Some lands on rocky soil. It takes root and begins to grow but the roots do not go down deep enough into the ground and the young plants are scorched by the sun. This seed represents young Christians who begin the journey but 'believe only for a while and in a time of testing fall away'. Other seed falls among thorns and the thorns choke the life from the seed as both grow up together. This seed represents those who 'as they go on their way are choked by the cares, riches and pleasures of life and their fruit does not mature'. 'But as for that in the good soil', concludes Jesus, 'these are the ones who, when they hear the word, hold it fast in an honest and good heart, and bear fruit with patient endurance' (Luke 8.4-15).

That quality of patient endurance commended by Jesus is one of the most valuable in the Christian life and is one which makes the difference between a person's faith being simply a leisure interest which they pursue for a while or lifelong discipleship. In another famous New Testament passage, the Letter to the Hebrews appeals to the same quality. The image used for the Christian is that of the long-distance runner in the stadium: the crowd are the Christians who have gone before us in the race.

> Therefore, since we are surrounded by so great a cloud
> of witnesses, let us also lay aside every weight and the sin
> that clings so closely, and let us run with perseverance the
> race that is set before us, looking to Jesus the pioneer and
> perfecter of our faith, who for the sake of the joy that
> was set before him endured the cross, disregarding its
> shame, and has taken his seat at the right hand of the
> throne of God. Consider him who endured such hostility
> against himself from sinners so that you may not grow
> weary and lose heart.
>
> Hebrews 12.1–3

A very important part of building this quality of perseverance
in every Christian is developing godly habits and disciplines of
worship, prayer and service which, like an athlete's training, build
the qualities and strength to sustain us in demanding times.

Wisdom

The Bible and the Christian tradition are full of godly wisdom on
ways of living well and ways of addressing particular times of
difficulty. Some of this wisdom we will read and absorb for ourselves
in the context of worship and Christian fellowship and as we read
the Scriptures. But we all need the support of other Christians in
times of particular crisis, especially those who are gifted in pastoral
care and wisdom, whether they are ordained or lay. Sometimes help
is given simply through providing a listening ear. Sometimes we are
given a fresh sense of perspective. At other times, when we don't
know where to turn or what to do, a fresh sense of direction and
hope will become clear as we talk with others. In some situations it
may be that the way we are living or choices we have made have
played a part in causing the difficulty or pain.

For many people in these situations, our instincts are simply to
struggle on alone. We don't want to be a nuisance to anyone. Often
the wise thing is to seek help and support within the Christian

community. Christians are called to share one anothers' burdens (Galatians 6.2). As others make their care and wisdom available to us, so we in turn may be able to care for others as they pass through their own times of trial.

Transfiguration

Most of us will be able to think of people we know who have suffered a great deal in different ways and have been able to find, through their suffering, a way of grace and even of growth. Through pain or grief they have somehow been able, by the grace of God, to become deeper and better human beings: more at peace with the world; with a greater sense of perspective; with more time and compassion for the suffering of others; with a deeper sense of thankfulness and joy for the gifts each day brings. Other people, who may not have suffered to the same degree, never seem to escape from their suffering and difficulty: their souls become prisoners of self-pity, grief or bitterness. Their horizon shrinks to their immediate world. They become demanding people to be with, drawing energy and attention endlessly to themselves.

The deepest challenge in the times of difficulty we will face in our lives lies in this area of overcoming suffering: through all of the pain and difficulty, discovering the deeper thread of joy which lies beneath it all. The path of transfiguration, as we have seen, is not the path of denial: it begins with honesty and with acknowledging pain. Yet it leads on from honesty to healing and resolution of the inner scars of turmoil through being open to forgive and to move on. The death of Jesus Christ on the cross was an experience of the utmost desolation and agony. Yet that death and defeat was followed on the third day by a most glorious and joyous resurrection. The joy is deeper than the pain. Good Friday is followed by Easter Day.

Readings and prayers

How long, O Lord? Will you forget me for ever?
How long will you hide your face from me?
How long must I bear pain in my soul
and have sorrow in my heart all day long?
How long shall my enemy be exalted over me?

Psalm 13.1-2

Hear my prayer, O Lord;
let my cry come to you.
Do not hide your face from me
in the day of my distress.
Incline your ear to me;
answer me speedily when I call.
For my days pass away like smoke,
and my bones burn like a furnace.
My heart is stricken and withered like grass;
I am too wasted to eat my bread.
Because of my loud groaning
my bones cling to my skin.
I am like an owl of the wilderness,
like a little owl of the waste places.
I lie awake;
I am like a lonely bird on the housetop.

Psalm 102.1-7

My heart is in anguish within me,
the terrors of death have fallen upon me,
Fear and trembling come upon me,
and horror overwhelms me.
And I say, 'O that I had wings like a dove!
I would fly away and be at rest;
truly I would flee far away;
I would lodge in the wilderness.'

Psalm 55.4-7

I believe in the sun even when it does not shine.
I believe in love even when I do not feel it.
I believe in God even when He is silent.

Inscription on the walls of a cellar in Cologne,
Germany, where Jews hid from the Nazis

O God,
I try and think about you
but I can't see your face.
I try and talk to you,
but you don't answer me.
How can I know you love me
unless I feel your touch?
And how can I reach out to you
if you have gone away?
I want to understand you,
but you are too hard for me;
so I am waiting here in the dark,
waiting for you, O God.

Janet Morley

Lead us not into temptation
But deliver us from evil.

The Lord's Prayer

To choose Christ is to choose the cross . . . the way to
union with Jesus is not by acquiring possessions, not
even spiritual ones, not by building up but by letting
everything go.

Elizabeth Ruth Obbard

Lord God,
whose blessed Son our Saviour
gave his back to the smiters
and did not hide his face from shame:
give us grace to endure the sufferings of this
   present time
with sure confidence in the glory that shall be revealed;
through Jesus Christ our Lord.

The Christian Year: Collects and Post Communion Prayers
for Sundays and Festivals (Fourth Sunday of Lent)

Before I take the body of my Lord,
Before I share his life in bread and wine,
I recognize the sorry things within –
These I lay down.

The words of hope I often failed to give,
The prayers of kindness buried by my pride,
The signs of care I argued out of sight:
These I lay down.

The narrowness of vision and of mind,
The need for other folk to serve my will,
And every word and silence meant to hurt:
These I lay down.

Of those around in whom I meet my Lord,
I ask their pardon and I grant them mine,
That every contradiction to Christ's peace
Might be laid down.

Lord Jesus Christ, companion at this feast,
I empty now my heart and stretch my hands,
And ask to meet you here in bread and wine
Which you lay down.

                                        The Iona Community

Finally, be strong in the Lord and in the strength of his power. Put on the whole armour of God so that you may be able to stand against the wiles of the devil.

Ephesians 6.10-11

12
Christian Hope

See, I am making all things new!

Revelation 21.5

Then we shall be still and see;
we shall see and we shall love;
we shall love and we shall praise.
Behold what will be, in the end, without end!
For what is our end but to reach that kingdom which
has no end?

Augustine, *City of God*, XXII.30

The journey of our lives has a beginning in our conception and birth. The outward, physical journey of our lives has an ending: one day we shall die. As we have seen, the journey of our Christian faith has a beginning and baptism is a sign of that new birth. For the whole of our lives we are pilgrims and travellers: a people on a journey together. What is the destination? Where are we going?

The drama of creation

The destiny and destination of men and women has to be seen as part of the drama which is taking place within the whole of creation. According to the Bible the whole of the universe is created by God. The universe had a beginning. Despite its great beauty, the created universe is deeply flawed. Just as human beings are deeply flawed and our fault lines run through all we do, so those faults and failings and distortions in humanity run through and affect the whole creation.

God loves his creation and his purpose is to work within all he has made to redeem and to recreate where things are spoiled and distorted. At the centre of the renewing and remaking of creation is the birth and life, death and resurrection of Jesus, the Son of God. In Christ, God becomes part of his world to work from within and to transform. Through Christ's death on the cross, not only humanity but the whole creation begins to be healed and rescued from destruction. There is a remaking. One day, we believe, there will be a new heaven and a new earth and one day we shall share in that new heaven and earth as our life with Christ continues beyond and after death:

> Then I saw a new heaven and a new earth: for the
> first heaven and the first earth had passed away, and
> the sea was no more. And I saw the holy city, the new
> Jerusalem, coming down out of heaven from God,
> prepared as a bride adorned for her husband. And
> I heard a loud voice from the throne saying:

'See, the home of God is among mortals.
He will dwell with them as their God;
They will be his peoples,
and God himself will be with them;
he will wipe away every tear from their eyes.
Death will be no more;
mourning and crying and pain will be no more,
for the first things have passed away.'

Revelation 21.3-4

Pictures of eternal life

In almost every civilization, human beings have longed for life to continue beyond death. Many of the wonders of the world were built as some kind of attempt to escape death or to prepare for the life which might follow. Despite the pain and difficulty, there is so much which is good in this life and we do not want to let go. As one Old Testament writer says, 'You have put eternity into their minds'. We naturally reach out for life beyond death.

Because of the resurrection of Jesus, that longing becomes a sure and certain hope. Jesus died and rose again, the first fruits of the harvest of the dead. Because of his own resurrection, we know that Jesus' promise of eternal life to all who receive his gift is real and is to be trusted. The power of death over humanity has been broken. We can hope for more. But how can we describe eternal life?

As with many things which are beyond a literal description, the Bible and Christian writers through the centuries have used images and pictures to give us a sense of heaven. The garden is one such image. The picture of a great banquet or party is common in the gospels (comforting for those of us who enjoy our food and drink!). The service of Holy Communion is a foretaste of the heavenly banquet. Jesus uses the image of a welcoming house with many rooms. The Book of Revelation, as we have seen, has a picture of a great city coming down from heaven with God in the midst and dwelling among his people. The Letter to the Hebrews speaks of the promised land and Sabbath rest for the wandering people of God. In trying to describe the resurrection body we might have, Paul draws a parallel with a seed and what grows from it: you can't tell from looking at the seed what the eventual plant might be like. So you cannot tell from looking at our frail, temporary bodies now what the resurrection body might be like.

We can say with full assurance that, whatever heaven will be like, it will be at least a hundred times better than the best we can imagine. We will be caught up into the life of God. All that is good on earth will be found in heaven. All that is harmful or difficult or which destroys on earth will not be found in heaven (including those parts of us which hurt and damage others or ourselves). We will be individuals there but part of the wider community of the whole people of God. We will be reunited with those we have loved and from whom we have been separated by death and with Christians from the past who have watched over our journey. We will have answers to the questions which we have long wrestled with in this life. Our chief activity will be the worship and appreciation of God and celebration together.

> For now we see in a mirror, dimly, but then we will see face to face. Now I know only in part; then I will know fully, even as I have been fully known.
>
> 1 Corinthians 13.12

Eternal not everlasting

In Christ, our life with God is indeed without an end. But it is not enough to describe our inheritance as everlasting life which begins when we die. Jesus' promise to us is, rather, eternal life: life in a new dimension. That eternal life does not begin with death but, rather, begins with faith in Jesus Christ. That life is to be life in all its fullness (John 10.10), embracing the good things of creation as well as the call to costly discipleship.

Hope not fear

Sometimes teaching about the Christian faith in different periods of Church life has distorted our picture of God and of the last things so as to make us afraid of God rather than looking forward to seeing him face to face. This is especially the case whenever the Church has stressed judgement and the danger of being cast into eternal oblivion or, worse still, everlasting punishment if we commit certain sins.

There is a proper sense within Scripture and Church teaching that part of being human is taking responsibility for our lives, our choices, our actions and our words and that when we come face to face with God, we will have to give account of our lives and of our stewardship. There is certainly a strong element in Christian teaching which emphasizes that freedom of choice is also an essential part of being human: that no-one can be forced to accept God's gift of forgiveness or of eternal life. Yet both of these elements must be seen against the wider background of the character of God as revealed in Jesus Christ: the God who desires to heal not to hurt; to bind up not to tear down; to forgive rather than to punish; to create, recreate and build again rather than to destroy.

If heaven is like coming home, one of the most vivid pictures of homecoming in the Scriptures is the return of the prodigal son in the story Jesus tells in Luke 15. The younger son has realized his foolishness and wrongdoing. As he arrives home, fearing his father's anger yet throwing himself on his mercy, he does indeed give an account of all that he has done wrong. For all that this younger son has ignored him all these years, the Father is looking out for him; runs to greet him; welcomes him and embraces him; calls for a ring for his finger and shoes for his feet; a robe for his back and rejoices to welcome this son who was dead back into the family. There are many in this life who come home to God in that way. We may dare to hope and believe there will be such homecomings in heaven. The God who loves the world so much that he gives his Son for its redemption will stop at nothing to reveal his love to those in need.

Now and not yet

As Christians we are privileged to live in the time of human history which is after the death and resurrection of Jesus when the central acts of the great drama of redemption have been completed; death has been conquered; the Spirit has been given to the people of God and the Church herself has been called into being. However, we are also called to live in the time of 'not yet': the world, as we have seen, is still deeply flawed and sin and suffering are part of the experience of every Christian. The Bible tells us that this great era of 'now but not yet' will come to an end suddenly and without warning as Christ returns in power and majesty, bringing in his kingdom. Every generation of Christians has lived with the hope and expectation that Christ's return may be in their own lifetime. We are called by Jesus to be ready for that moment throughout our lives: but also to hold that readiness in tension with the normal day-to-day and year-to-year rhythm of living.

Sustained by hope

So we are called as Christian people to travel on with Jesus. Our journey will sometimes be very joyful: it will not be difficult to rejoice, to enjoy and appreciate Christian fellowship and worship; to be fulfilled in the Christian service to which we are called. Our journey will sometimes be very hard: uphill, against the wind. We will grow tired and want to stop or turn aside. In those times especially we will need to be sustained by the hope to which we are called: we have been given the gift of eternal life through Jesus Christ. We are citizens of heaven, travelling home.

Readings and prayers

Blessed are they who are invited to the marriage supper of the Lamb.

Revelation 19.9

A priest started a homily at a funeral saying: 'I am
going to preach about judgement.' There was dismay
in the congregation. Then he went on: 'Judgement
is whispering into the ear of a merciful and
compassionate God the story of my life which
I have never been able to tell . . . what a relief it will
be to be able to whisper freely and fully into that
merciful and compassionate ear. After all, that is
what he has always wanted. He waits for us to come
home to Him.'

Basil Hume

Almighty God,
you have made us for yourself,
and our hearts are restless till they find their
    rest in you:
pour your love into our hearts and draw us
    to yourself,
and so bring us at last to your heavenly city
where we shall see you face to face;
through Jesus Christ your Son our Lord,
who is alive and reigns with you,
in the unity of the Holy Spirit,
one God, now and for ever.

*The Christian Year: Collects and Post Communion Prayers for
Sundays and festivals* (Seventeenth Sunday After Trinity)

If you have been raised with Christ, seek the things
that are above, where Christ is seated at the right
hand of God. Set your minds on the things that are
above, not on the things that are on the earth, for you
have died, and your life is hidden with Christ in God.
When Christ who is your life is revealed, then you also
will be revealed with him in glory.

Colossians 3.1-4

Give rest, O Christ, to your servant with your saints:
where sorrow and pain are no more, neither sighing,
but life everlasting.
You only are immortal, the creator and maker of life:
And we are mortal, formed of the earth, and to the
earth we shall return:
For so you did ordain when you created me, saying
Dust you are, and to dust you shall return.
All we go down to the dust; and weeping at the grave
we make our song:
Alleluia, Alleluia, Alleluia.

Russian Contakion of the Departed

A prayer for those who mourn

We remember, Lord, the slenderness of the thread
which separates life from death, and the suddenness
with which it can be broken.

Help us also to remember that on both sides of that
division we are surrounded by your love.

Persuade our hearts that when our dear ones die
neither we nor they are parted from you.

In you we may find peace, and in you be united with
them in the body of Christ, who burst the bonds of
death and is alive for evermore, our Saviour and theirs
for ever and ever.

Dick Williams

Happy and wise are they who endeavour to be during
their life as they wish to be found at their death.

Thomas à Kempis

Brothers and sisters, join in imitating me, and observe
those who live according to the example you have in
us. For many live as enemies of the cross of Christ;
I have told you of them, and now I tell you even with
tears. Their end is destruction; their god is the belly;
and their glory is in their shame; their minds are set
on earthly things. But our citizenship is in heaven, and
it is from there that we are expecting a Saviour, the
Lord Jesus Christ. He will transform the body of our
humiliation so that it may be conformed to the body
of his glory, by the power that also enables him to
make all things subject to himself. Therefore, my
brothers and sisters, whom I love and long for, my
joy and my crown, stand firm in the Lord.

Philippians 3.17–4.1

My mind was lifted up to heaven and I saw our Lord
as a lord in his own house where he had called his
much-loved friends and servants to a banquet. I saw
that the Lord did not sit in one place but ranged
throughout the house, filling it with joy and gladness.
He himself, courteously and companionably, greeted
and delighted his dear friends with love shining from
his face like marvellous melody that has no end. It is
this look of love shining from God's face that fills the
heavens full of joy and gladness.

Julian of Norwich

May the road rise to meet you.
May the wind be always at your back.
May the sun shine warm upon your face.
May the rain fall softly on your fields
Until we meet again.
May God hold you in the hollow of his hand.

A Gaelic blessing

An Order for Daily Prayer

Preparation

In the morning

Almighty and everlasting Father,
we thank you that you have brought us safely
to the beginning of this day.
Keep us from falling into sin
or running into danger;
order us in all our doings;
and guide us to do always
what is right in your eyes;
through Jesus Christ our Lord. Amen.

Common Worship

In the evening

Lighten our darkness,
Lord, we pray,
and in your mercy defend us
from all perils and dangers of this night;
for the love of your only Son,
our Saviour Jesus Christ. Amen.

Common Worship

The Word of God

One or more readings from the Bible.

Reflection upon the readings.

Prayers

Our Father in heaven,
hallowed be your name,
your kingdom come,
your will be done,
on earth as in heaven.
Give us today our daily bread.
Forgive us our sins
as we forgive those who sin against us.
Lead us not into temptation
but deliver us from evil.

For the kingdom, the power and the glory are yours
now and for ever. Amen.

Common Worship

Other prayers

A prayer of dedication

Almighty God,
we thank you for the gift of your holy word.
May it be a lantern to our feet,
a light to our paths,
and a strength to our lives.
Take us and use us
to love and serve
in the power of the Holy Spirit
and in the name of your Son,
Jesus Christ our Lord. Amen.

Common Worship

Further Reading

Twenty books to help keep you travelling well:

Carlo Carretto, *Letters from the Desert,* Darton, Longman &
Todd, 1972.

Stephen Cottrell, *Praying through Life,* Church House Publishing, 1998.

Gordon Fee and Douglas Stewart, *How to Read the Bible for all its
Worth,* Scripture Union, 1994

Richard Foster, *Celebration of Discipline,* Triangle, 1980.

George Guiver, *Everyday God,* Triangle, 1994.

Joyce Huggett, *Listening to God,* Hodder, 1986.

Gerard Hughes, *God of Surprises,* Darton, Longman & Todd, 1985.

Basil Hume, *Searching for God,* St Bede's Publications, 2000.

Julian of Norwich, *Revelations of Divine Love,* Penguin Classics, 1966.

C.S.Lewis, *The Screwtape Letters,* Fount, 1942.

Gordon MacDonald, *Ordering your Private World,* Highland, 1984.

Michael Marshall, *Free to Worship,* Fount, 1996.

Henri Nouwen, *The Return of the Prodigal Son,* Darton, Longman &
Todd, 1994.

Michael Ramsey, *Be Still and Know,* Fount, 1982.

Rule for a New Brother, Darton, Longman & Todd, 1973.

John Stott, *Basic Christianity,* IVP, 1958.

Thérèse of Lisieux, *The Story of a Soul: Autobiography of a Saint,* Fount,
1958.

Thomas à Kempis, *The Imitation of Christ,* Penguin Classics, 1952.

W.H.Vanstone, *Love's Endeavour, Love's Expense,* Darton, Longman &
Todd, 1977.

Robert Warren, *Living Well,* Fount, 1999.

References

William Abraham, *The Logic of Evangelism*, Hodder &
Stoughton, 1989

The Book of Common Prayer, Cambridge University Press.

Dietrich Bonhoeffer, *Ethics*, SCM Press, 1995

Mgr Michael Buckley (ed.), *A Treasury of Catholic Prayer*,
Kevin Mayhew, 1979.

Anthony P. Castle (ed.), *Quotes and Anecdotes*, Kevin
Mayhew, 1979.

*The Christian Year: Collects and Post Communion Prayers
for Sundays and Festivals*, Church House Publishing, 1997.

Frank Colquhoun (ed.), *Contemporary Parish Prayers*, Hodder
& Stoughton, 1975.

Common Worship: Daily Prayer, Church House Publishing, 2002.

Common Worship: Initiation Services, Church House Publishing, 1998.

*Common Worship: Services and Prayers for the Church
of England*, Church House Publishing, 2000.

Lucien Deiss, *Biblical Prayers*, World Library Publications, 1976.

Lucien Deiss, *Come Lord Jesus*, World Library Publications,
1976, 1981.

The Epistle to Diognetus, translated by Henry Meecham, Manchester
University Press, 1949.

Richard Giles, *We Do Not Presume: A Beginners Guide to
Anglican Life and Thought*, Canterbury Press, 1998.

John Gilling and Sister Patricia (eds), *When You Pray*, Darton,
Longman & Todd, 1978.

George Herbert, *The Country Parson, The Temple*, edited by
John W. Wall, SPCK, 1981.

Basil Hume, *To Be a Pilgrim*, St Paul's Publications, 1984.

Julian of Norwich, *Revelations of Divine Love*, translated by Clifton Wolters, Penguin, 1966.

John Keble, *The Christian Year*, SPCK, 2002.

The Methodist Service Book, Methodist Publishing House, 1975.

Mother Teresa of Calcutta, *In the Silence of the Heart*, SPCK, 1983.

New Patterns for Worship, Church House Publishing, 2002.

Henri Nouwen, *Reaching Out*, Doubleday, 1995.

Henri Nouwen, *In the Name of Jesus: Reflections on Christian Leadership*, Darton, Longman & Todd, 1997.

Elizabeth Ruth Obbard, *To Live Is To Pray: An Introduction to Carmelite Spirituality*, Canterbury Press, 1997.

Patterns for Worship, Church House Publishing, 1995.

Rule for a New Brother, Darton, Longman & Todd, 1973.

St Augustine, *The City of God*, translated by Henry Bettenson, Penguin Classics, 1972.

St Cyril of Jerusalem, 'On the Mysteries', in Maurice Wiles and Mark Santer (eds), *Documents in Early Christian Thought*, Cambridge University Press, 1975.

John Greenleaf Whittier, 'Dear Lord and Father of Mankind', *The Complete Celebration Hymnal*, Mayhew McCrimmon, 1984.

Dick Williams (ed.), *More Prayers for Today's Church*, Kingsway, 1984.